IN CLOSE HARMONY

IN CLOSE HARMONY

The Story of
the Louvin Brothers

Charles Wolfe

University Press of Mississippi   Jackson

Parts of this book first appeared, in a different form, as the annotations booklet to *Close Harmony* (BCD 15561), a compact disc set issued by Bear Family Records in 1992. They are used here by permission of Bear Family Records.

Library of Congress Cataloging-in-Publication Data

Wolfe, Charles K.
   In close harmony : the story of the Louvin Brothers / Charles Wolfe.
     p. cm. — (American made music series)
   Includes bibliographical references (p.) and index.
   ISBN 0-87805-891-5 (cloth : alk. paper). — ISBN 0-87805-892-3 (paper : alk. paper)
   1. Louvin Brothers. 2. Country musicians—United States—Biography. I. Title. II. Series.
   ML421.L7W65 1996
   782.42'1642'0922—dc20
   [B]   96-16708
                                                  CIP
                                                 MN

British Library Cataloging-in-Publication data available

CONTENTS

ACKNOWLEDGMENTS

This book originated as a set of annotations to a compact disc reissue of the complete commercial recordings of the Louvin Brothers, *Close Harmony*. The set of eight compact discs was issued by Germany's Bear Family Records (BCD 15561), under the production supervision of Richard Weize. (For information about the set, contact Bear Family Records, P.O. Box 1154, 2864 Vollersode, Germany.) The set also contains a complete Louvin Brothers discography. To Richard Weize I am grateful for his encouragement and suggestions.

I owe another major debt to Stephen Plumlee, who with his partner William Hogeland is developing a major film about the Louvins. I spent many hours talking with Stephen about the Louvins, and he graciously shared with me interviews he had conducted with Charlie Louvin and his circle. We also did a number of joint interviews with Charlie.

My greatest debt is to Charlie Louvin himself. He took hours from his busy schedule to talk with me and to let me look at his photos and scrapbooks. He was forthright, patient, and gracious, and this book could not have happened without him.

Working out the Louvin discography was a complicated and arduous task, and for help with it I am indebted to Gary B. Reid, who graciously shared with me his own early draft of the discography, and Eddie Stubbs, who listened carefully to the Louvin recordings and made dozens of valuable suggestions. Phillip Wells, who had for years been compiling a list of Louvin Brothers songs recorded by others, freely shared his research with me. Richard Weize was able to get and share information from the record company files.

Others who helped with various parts of the project include Susie Reed of Mountain Magic Talent, who set up appointments and interviews; Eddie Stubbs, who offered much good advice about Nashville in the 1950s; writers

Don Rhodes, Doug Green, Howard Miller, and others listed in the bibliography; Don Roy, who did an invaluable service by checking through the files of the Country Music Foundation archives for rare and important early fan magazine articles; Ronnie Pugh, Chris Skinker, and John Rumble who gave advice and help in locating research materials; Ken Nelson, Paul Yandell, Jimmy Capps, Goober Buchanan, Charles and Ida Whitstein, Ken Irwin, Sophie Tipton, Johnny Wright, Shot Jackson, Beecher Kirby, Larry Talbot, Grandpa Jones, Buddy Harman, John Hartford, Rich Keinzle, Don Cusic, and Hugh Cherry who contributed interviews and insights. I also want to thank the staff of The Center for Popular Music at Middle Tennessee State University in Murfreesboro and the research assistance of Stacey Wolfe. As always, my gratitude goes to my wife Mary Dean Wolfe and daughters Cindy and Stacey. Finally, I must thank JoAnne Prichard and her staff at the University Press of Mississippi for their encouragement, and David Evans and Colin Escott for reading the manuscript and making many constructive suggestions.

CKW
Murfreesboro, TN

DISCOGRAPHICAL NOTE

A detailed discography of all the Louvin Brothers commercial recordings is
not presented here, but starting in chapter 6 (the recordings of March 23,
1953—session 7, when the Louvin recordings start to play a major part in their
career), I have listed all the recordings on a session-by-session basis. All of these
recordings were made in Nashville on the various dates indicated. I have also
added the composer credits as they appeared on the original releases, and
the catalog number of the original releases only. Many Louvin sides were later
included on various LP compilations and reissued in other formats, such as the
45 rpm "extended play" albums. More recently, many have made their way onto
compact disc. I have cited none of these later releases. The true Louvin devotee
wanting these, as well as complete listings of personnel and master numbers,
should consult the discography included with the Bear Family CD set *Close
Harmony* (BCS 15561, vol. 3). That effort is the work of Eddie Stubbs, Gary B.
Reid, Richard Weize, and myself.

CKW

Working out a new
song, ca. 1958

INTRODUCTION

In the summer of 1995, the well-known San Francisco songwriter and fiddler Laurie Lewis released a compact disc entitled *The Oak and the Laurel*. Although Lewis had been best known as an avant-garde bluegrass star and championship fiddler, this was an album of mellow, old-time duets. Singing with her was her friend and partner Tom Rozum, and in her liner notes Lewis explained that the album was a sort of therapy, part of their recuperation from an auto accident that nearly had killed them and other members of their band the year before. "The idea for this project has been in our thoughts for many years, but it seems like we've always had good reasons to put it off," wrote Lewis. The wreck changed that. As the pair recovered from their injuries, they began working in a studio at Pacheo, California, singing old familiar songs by the Carter Family, Bill Monroe, and the Everly Brothers. It was music that spoke to the heart, not the head; it was healing music.

One of the first songs on the album was "My Baby Came Back," a song penned in 1958 by a team of Alabama songwriters named Charles and Ira Louvin. "We couldn't imagine recording a duet album without including a song from the Louvin Brothers," Laurie explained. Left unsaid was the process by which a song crafted by two singers from a remote southern mountain area, working in the most commercial of all country music venues (Nashville and the Grand Ole Opry) could survive through the years and so touch a complex young San Francisco artist four decades later.

But in fact, there were abundant signs that the music of this one special team of Charles and Ira Louvin was touching people all over the country in a variety of ways in this summer of 1995. The summer marked the thirtieth anniversary of the sudden death of Ira Louvin in a car crash in Missouri and the irrevocable end to the Louvin Brothers' career. Around the country, there were few formal attempts to commemorate the event; there were no special concerts, no Grand Ole Opry tributes, no attempt on the part of the record companies to reissue memorial albums. But the music itself was still being heard and played—perhaps the best tribute of all.

In a suburb of Washington, D.C., bright young professionals gathered at The Birchmere to listen to their favorite bluegrass band, the Country Gentlemen, sing their famed version of the Louvins' "Love and Wealth." In Boston, Rounder Records began shipping copies of a release by a young Louisiana duo, the Whitstein Brothers, who had modeled their entire act on Louvin harmony, and whose latest CD was an entire set composed of nothing but Louvin gospel songs. In Nashville, a crowd at a private party surrounded singer Emmylou Harris, who picked up a borrowed guitar and started a lilting version of "If I Could Only Win Your Love," a 1958 Louvin song that she had made into a new hit in 1975. At a local Tower record store in Los Angeles, fans of the 1960s folk-rock group the Byrds marveled at the new CD reissue of their old *Sweetheart of the Rodeo* album with its reading of the Louvins' "The Christian Life." In Cleveland, a pair of fifteen-year-old girls, standing at an interactive station at the brand new Rock and Roll Hall of Fame, looked at a panel featuring The Everly Brothers. Under "Influences" was the name LOUVIN BROTHERS, and one of the girls pushed the dot by the name. The strains of "Take the News to Mother" filled the cubicle. "Oh wow," one of them said.

On the Grand Ole Opry that summer (the new Opry that was some ten miles out in the country from the old Ryman Auditorium where the Louvins had originally sung their songs), Charlie Louvin took his place on the world's longest-running radio show. Joined by a young couple named Steve and Debbie Wilkinson in place of Ira, with his own voice huskier and mellower with age, Charlie reached back into the past for a Louvin version of "How Great Thou Art." Across town later that week Kathy Louvin, Ira's daughter, appeared on an early morning TV show, talking about her recent hit for Ricky van Shelton, "Keep It Between the Lines." She explained to a skeptical reporter that, indeed, her father had been one of the Louvin Brothers, and that she had apparently inherited some of his talent. She then sang a song she had made up on the spot about whether or not the Houston Oilers football team might move to Nashville.

Although the Louvin Brothers had a career that really included only eight years in the national limelight, they made their music count. Historian Bill Malone, writing in the authoritative *New Grove Dictionary of American Music* declared that the Louvins were "probably the greatest traditional country duo in history." Elvis Presley, who toured with them, declared that his mother had owned all their records, and that he preferred their music to rock and roll. Bluegrass pioneer Bill Monroe, who sang at Ira's funeral, admitted that Ira was one of the two great tenor singers—the other being himself. Johnny Cash, at the tender age of twelve, came to a Louvin Brothers show to get autographs. Not long after she came to Nashville, Emmylou Harris visited the record archives at the Country Music Foundation and asked them to make tapes for her of the fragile old Louvin 78s. Bluegrass bands, for whom high, clear harmony has a special meaning, trade old Louvin songs like rare coins. Marty Stuart, the versatile young singer whose tastes range from family gospel to "hillbilly rock," has said, "The songs and harmonies of the Louvin Brothers still ring as loud and clear after all these years as they did when they were first recorded. Every time I need a shot of heaven, I go and listen to 'You're Running Wild.'"

Born in the 1920s, Ira and Charles Louvin grew up during the Depression in a remote part of northern Alabama known as Sand Mountain. Here they were nourished on the area's rich tradition of southern gospel music, and here they heard on the radio the popular duet singers of the time. For country music, it was the great age of duet singers, with acts like the Monroe Brothers, the Callahan Brothers, Karl and Harty, Wiley and Gene, and the Blue Sky Boys dominating the scene. By the 1940s, the Louvins knew that they too wanted to sing this sort of music, but by the time they worked their way through their own radio apprenticeship, tastes in music had changed. Honky-tonk singers like Hank Williams and slick cowboy singers like Gene Autry were setting the trends, and "harmony singing" usually meant the smooth, well-modulated pop stylings of groups like the Sons of the Pioneers. Ironically, the year the Louvins made their first MGM records, 1951, was the same year the Blue Sky Boys, perhaps the greatest of the older duos, announced their retirement.

Yet the Louvins never really thought of trying any other type of music. Dogged with a bizzare series of setbacks and frustrations, they still managed to get their music before the public and into the country music mainstream. At first, skeptical record producers tried to confine them and their rich harmonies to the genre of gospel music, but the brothers fought through this resistance. Buoyed by Ira's talent for songwriting, and with an excellent backup band, they developed their own style and single-handedly returned duet singing to the mainstream of commercial country music.

To be sure, the Louvin music was not a carbon copy of the duet singing of the past. The pair did indeed use the classic duet instrumentation—the simple mandolin and guitar—and they did have a repertoire that included older folk and sentimental songs. But they traded the soft, plaintive sound of the Blue Sky Boys and the Monroe Brothers for a more intense, piercing, full-throat harmony. It was their version of the classic "hard country" sound of Roy Acuff, Hank Williams, and Webb Pierce—a version of white southern soul music. They used for their backup not just the unamplified mandolin and guitar but the electric guitar, the fiddle, the bass, and even the drums. And they lent their harmony to a wide variety of new songs, from love anthems like "My Baby's Gone" to cheating songs like "You're Running Wild," from novelty songs like "Dog Sled" to rock and roll ballads like "On the Way to the Show." From their very first commercial recording in 1947 until their final Capitol session in 1963, they recorded a legacy of some 219 sides. By no means were all of them classics, but those that were changed the face of country music and reminded the country music world that there was still life in one of its most traditional styles.

This study is an attempt to trace the life stories of Ira and Charles Louvin, and how they struggled to get their music into the mainstream of country music. It explores the roots of that music and the details behind the songs they recorded. Of necessity, it deals with the personalities behind the music: Ira's volatile temper outbursts, his drinking, his womanizing; Charlie's attempts to understand the harsh realities of the music business, to deal with his brother's stormy creativity, to keep the act on an even keel. While this side of the story could have been sensationalized and dramatized, I have tried to keep the focus on the Louvin Brothers' art and on the work that survived the personality clashes. After the brothers agreed to split up in 1963, Charlie Louvin went on to have a vastly successful solo career as a Grand Ole Opry star. In the 1960s and 1970s he recorded more albums and had more chart hits on his own than the brothers did together, and this story needs also to be told. But the music Charlie Louvin crafted in these later years was in many ways quite different from that of the Louvin Brothers; he sought to establish his own style and succeeded in doing so. In this sense, his solo career lies beyond the real scope of this book.

To keep the focus on the art of the Louvin Brothers, then, a great deal of the book deals with Louvin songs and recordings; in other areas, I have relied on the personal recollections of Charlie Louvin, and of colleagues and

companions who knew both brothers. As far as I can tell, no one ever interviewed Ira Louvin at any length about his work or his songs; he emerges in
these pages through his songs and through the memories of those who were
fortunate enough to know him. When all is said and done, the special alchemy
that stoked his creative fires remains essentially a mystery—which, perhaps, is as
it should be.

IN CLOSE HARMONY

SAND MOUNTAIN

The most impressive geographical feature of northern Alabama is a place known as Sand Mountain. It's not really a mountain, but a huge plateau running for over a hundred miles in a southwest direction. It starts near the Georgia line and runs down near Rainsville and Albertville, through DeKalb and Blount counties, skirting the Tennessee River to the west, and winding up about thirty miles north of Birmingham. Up in the northeast part of the state, the plateau features rough, steep sides that discouraged early settlers, but after the Civil War the rich, sandy soil attracted settlers from nearby Georgia, from the Carolinas, and even from Tennessee. By the 1920s, the plateau was dotted with tiny communities like Jay Bird, Solitude, Hustleville, Flat Rock, Red Apple, Section, Harmony, and Double Bridges. The plateau farmers were somewhat isolated from the towns and valleys below, and they became self-reliant, independent, and proud. A 1984 article in a Birmingham newspaper noted the "unshakable sense of place" and "healthy respect for tradition" of the Sand Mountain people. Fiddling contests, dances, all-day singings, and Sacred Harp gatherings dominated the culture of the mountain. Writer Carl Carmer, in his *Stars Fell on Alabama*, described a singing on the mountain in 1934, at the depth of the Depression, in which over two thousand people were present. Only by then, too, had radios and record players begun to allow the newer forms of music to trickle into the villages on the plateau.

In the days just after World War I, a young man named Colonel Monero Allen Loudermilk came to the mountain from his original home in Murphy, North Carolina. His family had come from Germany in the late 1800s, and he was now looking for good land and elbow room. He found both in a little town called Section and he settled there. He soon met and courted Georgiane Elizabeth Wootten, daughter of a local Baptist preacher, and after a suitable

Louvin parents

time they were married. Like most farm couples in the 1920s, they wanted
a large family; rather, they needed one—hands to help work the cotton, the
cane, and the corn that were the cash crops. Eventually they had seven children,
five girls and two boys. The boys were christened Ira Lonnie and Charles Elzer
Loudermilk. Ira was older by almost three years; he was born April 21, 1924,
his brother Charles on July 7, 1927.

Around 1929, the family moved to Henagar, about halfway between Scottsboro and Fort Payne, at the northeastern end of the mountain. It was here that
Ira and Charles really grew up, and where they lived the hard, rural life that
would later inspire so much of their music. The outside world didn't intrude
much here; a rare exception was in 1931, when the sheriff of nearby Jackson
County arrested for rape nine black youths who would become known as The
Scottsboro Boys. Their subsequent trial and retrial attracted national attention
and become a cause célèbre of the civil rights movement.

In general, though, when the boys were growing up in the 1930s, life on
the mountain hadn't changed much since the first settlers came. There was no
electricity (the Rural Electrification Administration didn't get onto the mountain
until 1948) and most of the plowing was done with mules. Colonel Loudermilk
(Colonel was his name, not any sort of rank) had about twenty-three acres

Ira (L) and Charlie at the Old Spring Hill School, Sand Mountain, ca. 1938

of cleared ground, and on it he grew an amazing number of crops. There was cotton, which the family took five miles to Rosalie to get ginned; a good year might yield one bale (five-hundred pounds) per acre, although the government said they could only plant five acres of cotton in those days. The cane produced syrup, and a lot of it they carried forty miles down the mountain to Chattanooga; on some trips they carried as many as a thousand buckets of sorghum, to be sold for twenty-five cents a bucket. On other occasions, the family gathered vegetables—okra and tomatoes—and took them down to Fort Payne to sell on the streets. In the early days, they did this by wagon, leaving home at two in the morning to get down to town by seven, when the stores opened. After an hour, they'd be sold out, and could start back home; by one that afternoon, the kids were back in the garden picking the produce for the next day's sale. "It was a sort of vicious circle," recalls Charlie. It soon became also something from which both boys wanted to escape.

In the 1930s, as Ira and Charlie were growing up, Sand Mountain was home to a rich variety of musical traditions. In the family itself, Colonel Loudermilk was a good old-time frailing banjo player, striking down hard with his thumb and forefinger, and occasionally singing along with his picking. The region was home for a number of fiddling contests and regular dances, and Colonel was a familiar figure at many of these; at times he went as far as Chattanooga to enter contests, and old-time musicians in the Chattanooga area remembered him as a boisterous musician who played with a forceful, driving style. Sand Mountain was a favorite tour route for early country music professionals, like Uncle Dave Macon and Sam McGee from Nashville's Grand Ole Opry, and the Skillet Lickers, the premier string band that worked out of Atlanta. The Skillet Lickers, headed by comic fiddler Gid Tanner and contest fiddler Clayton McMichen, were so popular on Sand Mountain that in 1930 they recorded a two-sided record called "Jeremiah Hopkins' Store at Sand Mountain." Released nationwide on Columbia, the skit poked good-natured fun at the isolated rural setting, the country store, and the practice of many bands of playing for "collection wages." But by this time Sand Mountain had its own string band that was winning regional fame: the Johnson Family String Band of Albertville. Founded around 1880, the band evolved over a number of years to the point that they were one of the most competent and versatile groups in the South. Their attempt to become recording stars in 1928 failed when they got into an argument with the Okeh Company about royalties, and none of their records were ever released. They were soon on the radio and were fixtures at all sorts of community events. They played at everything from high school football games to picnics at Pierce Lake. In 1925, a local paper advertised such a picnic by noting: "Fried chicken, cold drink stands, watermelons and best of all, one of the best bands in this section will furnish the music. . . . That's the Johnson band of Albertville. If you have never heard this band, you don't know what you've missed."

Georgiane Wootten Loudermilk, Ira and Charlie's mother, sang some of the old unaccompanied folk ballads like "The Knoxville Girl" and "Mary of the Wild Moor." These songs were traditional in the truest sense—both had actually originated in the British isles—but the solo grassroots singing repertoires in northern Alabama actually went far beyond this sort of song. In later years, folk song collectors like Ray Browne, traveling through Alabama, would note that, unlike the situation in the Appalachians or in eastern Kentucky, singers in Alabama also embraced many parlor and sentimental songs from the nineteenth century. These were pieces like "I'll Be All Smiles Tonight" and "What Is a Home without Love" (both of which the Louvins later recorded), which had been written, published, and copyrighted in the 1800s, but which had gone into oral tradition over the years. Although some of the original singers who first sang for first-generation collectors like Cecil Sharp in the 1915–1920 era made a clear distinction between the older songs and the new, by the late 1920s popular recording groups like the Carter Family had blurred that distinction. By the 1930s, when the Louvins were hearing their mother sing, both the old parlor songs and the old British ballads were pretty well confused in the folk imagination: both types were old, sad, lonesome songs, and both lent themselves to the high, keening harmonies the Louvins later featured. Many of these songs stayed with the brothers for years and became a core of their early repertoire.

Georgiane's family was also heavily involved in church singing, and especially in a style of singing called Sacred Harp. Drawing its name from a popular song-book compiled in 1844 by two Georgia Baptist singing teachers, B. F. White and Elisha King, the singing is characterized by the use of shape notes—notes whose shape, not the position on the staff, determines pitch. Throughout the nineteenth century, as shape notes lost favor in the North, rural communities throughout the South continued to use the old "fasola" shape note books. Curiously, the singings eventually ceased to be done as part of regular church services but were almost always held in churches. Singers at a gathering formed a hollow square, with each part represented by a side: the tenor part carried the melody, amplified by the bass, treble, and alto. In a refreshingly democratic display, different members—male and female, young and old—took turns leading the assembly. Most of the songs sung dated from the mid-nineteenth century or earlier, and it was customary to "vocalize" the first chorus of the song—that is, to sing it through by "note" (i.e., fa-sol-la-mi) instead of by word.

For several decades in the twentieth century, Sacred Harp singing was con-fined mainly to the rural areas of northern Alabama and Georgia. By the 1960s and 1970s, though, the music was undergoing a revival, and soon was being sung in college and university music departments and by urban singers in places like Washington and Philadelphia. This modern version of the Sacred Harp, gener-ally detached from the religious fervor that marks the rural singers, is polite, tame, well modulated, and a far cry from the surging, passionate, strident voices heard at a Sand Mountain singing. It is the difference between a well mannered folksinger like Joan Baez and an genuine mountain singer like Hazel Dickens. In 1959, folksong collector Alan Lomax traveled to the community of Fyffe, not far from Henagar, to record in stereo a summer singing. Eventually issued on LP as *White Spirituals from "The Sacred Harp"* (New World NW 205), these recordings amazed Charlie Louvin when he heard them recently. "That's exactly what it sounded like when Ira and I went to these singings when we were growing up."

Both the Woottens (Georgiane's maiden name) and the Haynes family (her grandmother's name) had been active in Sacred Harp work for generations, and scholars who study the development of the Sacred Harp singing style often devote entire paragraphs to the importance of the Haynes-Wootten family. The family tradition starts with Thomas and Rhoda Haynes, who moved to the mountain at the end of the nineteenth century, probably carrying a copy of *The Sacred Harp* with them in their wagon. The pair had a large family—fourteen children—and Thomas taught all of them how to read and sing from the book. Two of the daughters, Beulah and Rhoda, married two local brothers, Jesse and Charlie Wootten, and it is the children of these two branches that were to do so much toward carrying on the family singing heritage. Rhoda and Charlie became grandparents of the Louvins. Beulah and Jesse had seven children, and these formed the core of the extended family that still functions on the mountain today—all living within a thirty-mile radius of the ancestral home at Ider. For years, in fact, members of the Haynes-Wootten family have held their own Sacred Harp singing every year in the summer at Section—a combination of incredible food and incredible music. One of the family's singers, Chester, was featured on the 1990 PBS documentary "American Patchwork." And Buell Cobb, the leading historian of the Sacred Harp music, has written of them: "Hearing for the first time the Woottens sing—when they are at anything like full strength—is to come upon what seems like an almost elemental force. Beyond the power and natural beauty of their individual voices, what compels attention is the purity of their blended sound, an ardent pressing of the voices against the discipline of the music they know so well." Not surprisingly, such a description is a perfect account of the later sound of the Louvin Brothers—blended purity, passionately "pressing the envelope" of the song's melody. And not surprisingly, as boys Ira and Charlie often went to such singings and absorbed, in all kinds of subtle ways, the music they heard there—especially the high, straining, top-of-the-range harmonies. "If anyone really wants to hear where Louvin Brothers harmony came from," Charlie says, "all they have to do is listen to a session of Sacred Harp singing."

The Sacred Harp was only one part of the sacred singing tradition that nourished the Louvins on Sand Mountain. Another was the newer, seven-shape-note gospel tradition, or what some of the residents called "new-book" singing. It was so called because the singers used seven shape notes instead of the four of the Sacred Harp, and because it featured newly composed songs instead of the old pre-Civil War ones. This movement began in the Shenandoah Valley

shortly after the Civil War, with the activities of Aldine S. Kieffer and Ephraim
Ruebush, two men who had become friends in a Union prison camp. Such
singing was tied to "normal schools"—rural singing schools taught by traveling
teachers—and to "singing conventions," gatherings of all the singers of an area
to try out new songs published in small, paperback songbooks. By the turn
of the century, graduates of the Ruebush-Kieffer programs had started their
own publishing companies across the South from Virginia to Texas. The most
successful ones were those of James D. Vaughan (in Lawrenceburg, Tennessee,
just north of the Alabama state line) and Stamps-Baxter (in Chattanooga and
Dallas). In many areas, the new-book music had replaced the older Sacred Harp,
and by the time the Louvins came along, the book publishing companies were
using modern, aggressive sales techniques to promote their books. They were
sponsoring professional quartets who sang samples of the new songs in the new
books—which usually were published once a year and known as "newbacks"—
and were getting these quartets programs on the radio and recording contracts
with major companies. Some of the quartets were becoming so popular that
they were breaking away from the sponsoring companies and going out on their
own, like the new generations of country singers.

For reasons not entirely clear, Sand Mountain, and northern Alabama in
general, became even more of a bastion for this style of music than it had for
Sacred Harp. During the first half of the twentieth century, the region produced
more key figures in seven-shape music than did any other state except Texas.
One of the most influential of the singers, composers, and teachers was Thomas
Benjamin Mosley (1872–1927) of Albertville. A native of Georgia, he studied un-
der gospel pioneer A. J. Showalter, and began teaching his own normals on Sand
Mountain about 1896. He also served as a director and editor for the Showalter
Publishing Company for over thirty years, until his tragic death in an automobile
accident in 1927. One of Mosley's many students was J. R. (Pap) Baxter, from
Lebanon in DeKalb County. Beginning as a teacher of harmony and a songwriter,
Baxter soon found that his true talent lay in the business end of the music, and
in 1926 he formed a partnership with V. O. Stamps to create the Stamps-Baxter
Music and Printing Company, which eventually became the nation's largest. Many
of the best composers in the movement also came from northern Alabama:
W. Oliver Cooper, Vep Ellis, Eugene Wright, and V. O. Fossett.

During the 1920s, the Athens Music Company and the Ganus Brothers
Company (from Birmingham) published their own influential gospel songbooks
and sent their normal teachers into the remote areas of the state. The former

(Athens) was to have an especially potent impact on the rise of gospel music. One of its editors was G. T. Speer, yet another student of T. B. Mosley, who became patriarch of the nationally known singing Speer Family. In the 1930s, as he gradually brought the members of his family into his singing act, he broke away from the shelter of the music publishing companies and went out on his own. By 1941 the Speer Family had their own radio show in Montgomery (which aired each week just before Hank Williams's show), and in the 1950s they pioneered gospel music on television. (Two members of the family also helped back Elvis Presley on his first RCA Victor recording session in 1956.) C. A. Brock, who managed the Athens company, had a son named Dwight who became gospel's first great piano player. In 1927 he traveled to Atlanta with the Stamps Quartet to make one of the cornerstone records of southern gospel: "Give the World a Smile Each Day." It was to become a best-seller and inspire hundreds of young piano players to do more than just chord behind the quarters.

Another figure in the Athens company was W. S. Hess, whose son Jake was a child singing prodigy, appearing in public with his brothers when he was only five years old. By 1948 Jake was singing with the Statesmen and winning fans around the country; one of them was the young Elvis Presley, who once played one of Jake's records for a friend and commented, "Now you know where I got my style." Yet another Athens alumnus was Alton Delmore, who later won fame as one half of the Delmore Brothers on the Grand Ole Opry. Both Alton's mother Mollie and his uncle W. A. Williams wrote songs for the Athens company and helped teach the Delmores "the rudiments."

During the time the Louvins were growing up, most of the musicians from the area who had had any commercial success with their music were gospel groups like the Speers. Another such group was the quartet headed by John Daniel, born in 1906 at Boaz in Marshall County. In the 1930s he was leading a quartet for the James D. Vaughan Company, one that included, at various times, Jake Hess and another major gospel singer, Wally Fowler. By the 1940s they had made the break and landed a job at Nashville station WSM and the Grand Ole Opry—one of the first such groups to do so. Also from Marshall County (Albertville) was singer Bobby Strickland; born in 1920, he is considered by many to be the finest quartet tenor of modern times. He sang for a time with the Harmoneers and then with the Statesmen before he was killed in an accident in 1953. Because of these successes, the Sand Mountain town of Boaz has become known as a center for southern gospel singing, and even today "singings" are more frequent in Boaz than in any other place in the South. Snead State Community College in Boaz today houses a substantial archive and museum devoted to the Sand Mountain gospel tradition: thousands of the "*newback*" songbooks, photos, letters, posters, instruments, records, and radio transcriptions—one of the very few such collections in the country. It is a testimony to just how pervasive the sacred singing tradition was on the mountain, and how difficult it would have been for the Louvins to ignore it. It was a tradition that had already had an impact far beyond the slopes of the mountain, and one the Louvins would take even farther.

Oddly, though, neither Louvin brother ever learned to sing the shape notes from the printed page, nor did either ever learn any formal "rudiments" of gospel singing. Many other early duet acts, such as the Delmore Brothers and the Blue Sky Boys, did in fact learn to read music from various singing school teachers who roamed the South in those days. And in fact, when the brothers were ten or eleven or twelve, their father decided to send them to such a singing school. A local teacher was holding one and approached Colonel about sending the boys. Charlie recalls:

> This singing teacher went to Papa and said, "I know they sing pretty good, I've heard them in church, but they don't really know what they're doing. They need to go to my school, so I can teach them what they're doing." Of course, times were really tough back then, but Papa finally decided to. He promised the man, "Next summer when you have the next school, I'll send the boys." It cost twelve dollars to go the two weeks. Next summer came, and Papa gave us the twelve dollars; we knew where the place was, about three miles from the house, and we took off walking. There were a few other boys there being sent, so we all got together—but we never made it that first day. We just headed out to the woods, went by the store and got some cigarettes and candy and soda pop, and hid out in the woods until about time the school was out. Then we'd get on back to the house. This went on for two or three days. Then Papa ran into this singing teacher man and he said, "Colonel, I thought you were going to send your boys to the singing school." Of course, papa knew right then what had happened. When we came home that night, he asked us how singing school was. And then the whipping started. He whipped us for not going; he whipped us for lying; he whipped us for spending the money; he cleaned our plow good. And we never did go back to a singing school.

In spite of all this, Colonel was proud of the way his two young sons could harmonize with each other and began to think of ways to show them off. They sang the songs they had heard in church around the house, but both were too bashful to sing in public. Charlie recalls how they solved the problem. "When Papa insisted that we sing for the neighbors, we would get under the old-time metal bed, which was only fourteen or sixteen inches off the floor, and we'd put our rear ends together and sing. This way, you could let your head drop and look between your legs and see each other. This paid off later because it taught us to phase together without looking." Gradually the boys started singing duets in church at the Wednesday night meetings, experimenting with ways to swap lead and harmony to fit their changing voices.

CLOSE HARMONY

By the early 1930s, phonograph records had become another important source of music for Charlie and Ira. Records were still a relatively new medium; the first self-conscious "hill country" record had been made in 1923, only about ten years earlier, but the genre had grown with breathtaking speed. By 1928 every major record label had started some kind of "hillbilly" or "old-time music" series, and hundreds of different titles were available. The Depression dealt the industry a temporary setback, but by 1935 things were looking better. Some labels were selling cut-rate records through Sears Roebuck and Montgomery Ward mail-order catalogs, and through newly organized chain stores like Kresge and Woolworth's; the Victor company, which had sold its Carter Family records in the 1920s for seventy-five cents each, was now selling its budget Bluebird line for thirty-five cents each and its Montgomery Ward line at three for a dollar.

On the mountain, a man named Ed Watkins, who ran the local general store, special ordered records that Colonel and his sons wanted, charging them only his cost. Whenever Colonel went to Knoxville, he visited the big record store there and brought home his prizes. "Papa would come home with sometimes a dozen new records," Charlie recalled. "And whenever he got home—at five in the evening or twelve midnight or two in the morning—we'd have to listen to every one. Even if we got up out of bed. We'd wind up the graphaphone and put those old big 78s on it and listen to both sides of everything he brought home before we'd go back to bed. And that's where we got a lot of our material from." Colonel liked, not surprisingly, Uncle Dave Macon, the old-time banjoist and singer from Nashville's Grand Ole Opry; he was also partial to the Carter Family and, a little later, the gospel singing Chuck Wagon Gang from Texas. He loved things with harmony singing, even the later records by Roy Acuff, where Bashful Brother Oswald sang the "screaming tenor" on songs like "Precious Jewel." One artist he did not bring home on records was Jimmie Rodgers, the famed "blue yodeler." Neither Colonel nor his sons ever thought much of Rodgers and his music—possibly because so much of it was vocal solos. Ira and Charlie themselves soon found new heroes in the records of the Delmore Brothers and the Blue Sky Boys—especially the latter, since they could never pick them up on radio, and their records were the only way they could study their unique harmony.

The 1930s was country's great age of harmony singing, and many of the leading performers either featured or used exclusively close harmony singing styles. Not much is actually known about the origins and development of this style; country music historians have been very good about tracing the histories of songs and the biographies of performers, but less dedicated to tracing just where performing methods came from. In the case of "close harmony" singing—in which the tenor harmony is as close to the original melody as it can get—there were probably two sources: gospel music and various "schools for the blind" that flourished in the South in the early twentieth century. The old gospel songbooks published by companies like James D. Vaughan usually had songs arranged for four parts: two in the treble clef and two in the bass clef. The two parts written in the treble clef were almost always arranged in close harmony, often a third apart. There was also an early gospel tradition of accompanying such singing by the mandolin and guitar. In the early 1920s, a Texas team named Perry Kim and Einar Nyland recorded with mandolin and guitar for Homer Rhodeheaver's all-gospel Rainbow label, based in Chicago. Even earlier, before the turn of the century, there is evidence that mandolin and guitar accompaniments were being used at rural brush arbors and revivals where a piano or organ was not available. Researcher Harlan Daniel has found that prior to World War I Alva Thomas and another representative of the Quartet Music Company, a publisher in Fort Worth, were singing "specials" at singing conventions with mandolin and guitar backup.

As the 1920s spread radio throughout the South, listeners even in the most remote areas were exposed to a rich vein of pop and vaudeville music. From powerful stations in Chicago and New York (and later from the new networks) came the songs of Ford and Glenn (Ford Rush and Glenn Rowell) and the vaudeville-derived fare of Billy Jones and Ernest Hare, the Happiness Boys. (Their big hit was "Singing in the Bathtub.") These acts did not sound very country—they used a piano accompaniment and lots of Tin Pan Alley material—but they became favorites with many rural listeners.

People who were visually handicapped in the South at the turn of the century had relatively few options. In a time of poorly funded public education and misconceptions about the potential of blind students, one of the most common vocations for the blind was music. Many of the first generation of country musicians—that is, people who really sought to make a living from their music—were either partially or completely blind. They included the famed guitarist and singer Riley Puckett, singer George Reneau ("The Blind Minstrel of the Great Smoky Mountains"), fiddler and banjoist Dick Burnett, the team of McFarland and Gardner (Mac and Bob), legendary fiddler Ed Haley, composer and singer Andrew Jenkins, and composer-singer Alfred Reed. A surprising number of these performers had received some sort of musical training at various schools for the blind set up in Kentucky, Tennessee, Georgia, and other regions. This musical training was rather formal, and the manner of harmony singing taught there was rather stiff and polite. Some singers managed to overcome this training; others never did.

The first commercial recordings of a regular country duet act appears to have been made by a pair of obscure singers named Reuben Puckett and Richard Brooks. Until recently, little was known of them save that they recorded several times in Atlanta; now it appears that they were both blind, and that they lived in Knoxville. On January 29, 1925, only about eighteen months after Fiddlin' John Carson's "first" country record in 1923, Puckett (no relation to Riley Puckett) and Brooks accompanied themselves on fiddle and guitar as they sang two sentimental numbers, "Always Think of Mother" and "Down by the Mississippi Shore." The record was released in the Columbia Old Familiar Tunes series and sold well enough that the pair was called back to record again and to record for the rival Victor label. A couple of months later, in the spring of 1925, Frank and James McCravy, brothers from Laurens, South Carolina, fresh from the tent-revival circuit, went to New York to record the first duets by a real brother act for the Okeh label. By 1928, when A. P. and Sara Carter's "Little Darling Pal of Mine" on Victor became the first male-female country duet hit, the record catalogs were full of homespun duos trying out their harmony in the new medium.

The first really successful country duet act was a team known affectionately to generations as Mac and Bob. Their real names were Lester McFarland and Robert Gardner, and they were also one of the first acts really to make a living from their music. Gardner was born in Oliver Springs in north Tennessee, while McFarland came from across the state line in Gray, Kentucky. Both were blind from birth, and they met in 1915 at the Kentucky School for the Blind, where both received formal musical training. By 1922 they were performing together professionally, and in 1926 they traveled to New York to make their first records for the old Vocalion company. During the next five years, they recorded more than a hundred selections, putting them among the most often recorded of the early country singers. Their 1927 recording of "When the Roses Bloom Again," a 1901 sentimental song from Tin Pan Alley, became a huge hit, and over the years may have had sales approaching a million copies. The plaintive singing and delicate mandolin-guitar backing made the performance a standard for later duet acts. After local radio work and tours on the Keith-Albee vaudeville circuit, Mac and Bob went to radio station WLS in Chicago, where they became fixtures on "The National Barn Dance." There they stayed until Bob's retirement in the early 1950s.

Mac and Bob helped usher in the first great revolution in the robust infant art called country music. During the late 1920s, the older fiddle players, string bands, banjoists, and husky-voiced street-corner singers became passé, victims in part of the new technology of radio and the electrical recording system. The new stars included acts like Karl and Harty, Kentuckians who won fame over Chicago radio; Darby and Tarlton, who worked through Georgia and Alabama and sang "Columbus Stockade Blues" and "Birmingham Jail"; Fleming and Townsend, who applied the blues and blue yodels of Jimmie Rodgers to the duet style; the Callahan Brothers from North Carolina; and the team of Hugh Cross and Riley Puckett, who popularized "Red River Valley." Millie and Dolly Good, the Girls of the Golden West, applied the style to women's voices, and sang western songs over WLS. Most of the new acts made their mark on radio, and most of them were young, adaptable, and creative. Although many of the songs were older and conservative—or at least they sounded older and conservative—the singers were not. Alton and Rabon Delmore, who grew up in the shadow of Sand Mountain, were twenty-four and sixteen, respectively, when they started. Walter and Homer Callahan were twenty-three and twenty-one. Millie and Dolly Good were twenty and seventeen. Karl and Harty were older, at ages twenty-eight and twenty-seven. But the Blue Sky Boys, who were to become such an influence on the Louvins, first faced the microphones in 1935, when they were only fifteen and seventeen.

The themes and messages of the duet songs were unabashedly sentimental, nostalgic, and moralistic. The repertoire was full of old gospel songs, many adapted from the old shape-note songbooks. "As for what songs audiences liked best, I would say that the hymns possibly drew at least 50 per cent or more of

Early radio duet The Blue
Sky Boys (Bill and Earl
Bolick)

the requests," recalled Blue Sky Boy Bill Bolick. The first record hits for Karl
and Harty, the Monroe Brothers, and the Blue Sky Boys were all sacred songs.
Other duet favorites were old songs from folk tradition, nineteenth-century
composed songs, and newer songs modeled on them. Thus, these young sweet
southern voices sang of old log cabins, mother, tearful reunions, prisons, death,
murder, the green hills of Virginia, and the good old days.

Yet many of the young duet singers were far from naive country primitives,
blindly following their emotions and instincts. Good duet singing was a complex
and demanding skill, and its best practitioners were highly self-conscious and
deliberate craftsmen. Bill Bolick offered a detailed explanation of how—and
why—the Blue Sky Boys crafted their sound:

> Both of us realized from the very beginning that in order to produce a good, clear
> harmony, one had to sing at a moderate pace in order to be understood and softly

if your voices were to blend. From the first we strove to keep the harmony and the lead separate. We always tried to sing in our natural God-given voices. We didn't try to see how high we could sing or how loud we could sing. We tried to sing in a key that we felt would suit our voices best without yelling or straining. We didn't play our instruments loud. When it was necessary that the harmony reach a high pitch, I learned to reach these notes without increasing the volume of my voice, so that the sound that I attained wouldn't be any louder than Earl's lower-pitched voice.

Fortunately, the developing technology of the 1930s, especially the increased sensitivity of radio and recording microphones, made a smooth, blended sound like that of the Blue Sky Boys more viable. Ten years earlier the Blue Sky Boys or Karl and Harty or the Delmores could not have made it in either medium. Their voices would have been too soft for the older microphones or vaudeville stages. As country music historian Bob Coltman has written: "Old time music, 1920s style, had been shaped in the days of no microphones, when subtlety was lost in the ambient noise of schoolrooms and front porches, street corners and makeshift stages. By contrast, the radio, which could control its incidental noise to the vanishing point (static excepted), was hushed, intimate, the microphone's exclusiveness encouraging soft, expressive, modulated voices, music with nuance and suggestion."

Radio was also exploding in popularity across the South during this time. By 1926 radio receivers designed to run on household current became available, and in the 1930s, as more and more rural homes got electricity, the radio became the central piece of front-room furniture. With the deepening Depression, people turned more and more to the free entertainment of the radio. Broadcasting stations, too, were proliferating; a 1932 radio listening logbook listed 137 stations in the South and Southeast alone. For a time there was even a magazine called *Rural Radio* that catered to fans of country music programs and stars of interest to rural listeners.

Radio also offered many musicians their first chance to become full-time professionals. Some found they could eke out a living by using their regular radio spots to advertise personal appearances and sell songbooks. But it was barely a living. WSM, one of the biggest and most powerful clear-channel stations in the South, paid the Delmore Brothers fifteen dollars a week for doing the Grand Ole Opry and three weekly morning shows. The Callahan Brothers started at four dollars each per week at WWNC, Asheville. Young aspiring country singers often ran afoul of local musicians' unions, which sometimes barred

country pickers and singers from their ranks. Most radio performers had to
live a restless, nomadic existence, moving on after a year or two at one station
because they had "played out" the territory—that is, they had so saturated the
region with personal appearances that they no longer drew much fan mail and
could not attract crowds to their personal appearance shows. Working within
such constraints, larger string bands of four or five pieces could not survive—
but two brothers in a beat-up old Ford could make do.

There were more personal, visceral reasons for the popularity of duet music. It suited almost perfectly the need of its audience—or a large part of it.
Considerably expanded beyond the one that bought the first country records
in the 1920s, this audience now included a lot more poor people, older people,
and women for whom slow, sentimental songs and personal touches had great
appeal. The songs of nostalgia and sentiment and orphan children and old times
also offered escape from the harsh realities of the Depression. While city folk
sought escape in Hollywood spectacles such as *King Kong* or *Flying Down to
Rio*, their rural counterparts found comfort in the emotion of "The Prisoner's
Dream" or the pathos of "The Orphan Girl" (about a little girl who freezes
to death on the steps of a rich man's door). And the fans were grateful. "As
long as you are on the air and I'm listening you'll always have a loyal fan in me,"
one ardent fan wrote Millie and Dolly Good in 1934. "I hope I have made you
understand my feelings because I cannot put my true thoughts on paper."

Such was the nature of the potent brother duet tradition with which the
Louvins grew up; although they did not make the big time until the tail end of
this tradition, its qualities both informed and inspired them. They were to explore its directions, honor its originators, and struggle with its limitations; in the
end, though, they were to take it to new heights and forge for it a permanent
place in modern country music.

The Delmore Brothers were special to Ira and Charlie as well as most of the
people on Sand Mountain, since they were Alabama natives who had grown up
only a couple of counties to the west. Indeed, one of the best-known Delmore
songs was an original called "Sand Mountain Blues." In the 1930s, the Delmores
began recording regularly for the Bluebird label and were heard almost daily
on the radio. They had joined the Grand Ole Opry in 1933, and in those days
WSM's 50,000-watt signal could be picked up easily on the mountain. The
problem was that not many on the mountain had radios; the first one the
brothers remembered was one owned by Ed Watkins, the storekeeper, and
many Saturday nights Ira and Charlie walked the quarter of a mile down the

Delmore Brothers in the mid-1940s, about the time they recorded "Sand Mountain Blues"

road to the Watkins house to listen to the Opry. Often they found as many as twenty people assembled in the Watkins living room, gathered around the battery-powered set, listening to the Solemn Old Judge introduce Uncle Dave Macon, The Vagabonds, the Fruit Jar Drinkers, Fiddlin' Arthur Smith, the Delmores, and, later on, young Roy Acuff. Sand Mountain etiquette required that if anyone wanted to talk during the show, they went out into the yard so as not to disturb others. Ira and Charlie knew just when the Delmore segment of the show came on, and they listened intently. They soon noticed that the Delmores were doing the same kind of thing they were trying to do with their singing—switching around the lead and harmony in the same arrangement. Later Colonel himself bought a battery-powered radio, but quickly taught the boys to limit the playing time to save batteries.

The Monroe Brothers, Bill and Charlie, were also important in these early years. Ira was especially fascinated by the Monroes' Bluebird recordings and (after 1939) by listening to Bill Monroe's mandolin playing on the Opry. Both boys liked the "high harmony" the Monroes had—harmony much higher and more

The Monroe Brothers,
Charlie (L) and Bill (R),
ca. 1937

dramatic than the bluesy, soft sound of the Delmores or the tight, midrange closeness of the Blue Sky Boys. (Later, the Louvin Brothers did a tribute album to the Delmores and planned follow-up tribute albums for the Monroes and the Blue Sky Boys; sadly, the latter two albums were never recorded.) Ira had been fascinated with instruments at an early age, and on occasion had borrowed his father's banjo to experiment; he even managed fairly good imitations of one of his father's favorites, Uncle Dave Macon. When he was eight, Ira made a homemade mandolin of sorts out of a syrup bucket and corn stalk, with waxed-up threads for strings. Later Ira traded an old bicycle for a beat-up guitar and began learning on a real instrument. The records they loved, though, all featured a mandolin, and soon Ira had decided that if he and Charlie were going to sound anything like the men they heard on the records, they had to have a mandolin and guitar backing. The occasional back-up their father offered on his claw-hammer banjo did not fit.

It wasn't until he was nineteen that Ira finally got his mandolin: an old Gibson F-12 he found in a pawn shop in Chattanooga. He immediately turned the guitar over to Charlie, then all of sixteen, and taught him the basic guitar chords so he could play rhythm. Then he set to work learning about the mandolin: over and over he played the Monroe Brothers records, copying each lick Bill did in the turnarounds and leads. As he paced back and forth across the floor, his head bowed to catch the music on the Victrola, his family began to get their first sense of the intensity of Ira's interest in music. Soon his intensity affected Charlie as well, and before long the two were overcoming their shyness and going out into the community to play in public. Charlie recalls: "We sang at every cakewalk, ice cream supper, or anything else anybody had to offer, for free."

The first time the brothers were actually paid for performing was on July 4, 1940, at a town called Flat Rock, about ten miles up the road from Henagar. "We sang in the center of a flying Jenny," said Charlie. "It was a sort of a home-made merry-go-round, and it was powered by mules. There were straight benches around it—you could even see the grass through the cracks in the platform. We sat right in the middle and sang." Every hour the boys would get a break, go get a drink to cool off, rest a bit, and then start in again. It went on all day, in a blazing Alabama summer, and at the end Ira and Charlie were paid three dollars each. They were impressed; "that three dollars was six times what our father could make working from daylight to dark on the farm." The idea of making money by playing their music was starting to take hold.

At about the same time, the brothers had their ambitions fueled by another lesson in professionalism: a local visit by Grand Ole Opry star Roy Acuff and his troupe. One night as Ira and Charlie listened to the Opry, they heard Acuff announce that he and his "boys and girls" were scheduled to play at the Spring Hill School in Henagar, Alabama. The boys were stunned. Not only was Spring Hill the very school they had attended, but from the way Acuff was coming, he would have to go right by their house. The day for the concert came, and the boys found themselves out hoeing in the field, keeping their eyes peeled on the dirt road that went by their house. It was late summer, and the road was dusty and hot. Suddenly they heard a noise in the distance, and a cloud of dust, and then a car came into view. Charlie remembers, "I'll be damned if there wasn't a car that looked to us as long as a three-quarter ton truck. I found out later it was an air-cooled Franklin. On the side were the words, 'Roy Acuff and the Smoky Mountain Boys.' I'd never seen anything like that." The boys had to continue their work in the fields until the sun went down, but then they took off to the school; both knew they had no chance of getting inside—there was an admission charge of twenty-five cents, which neither of them had—but they could stand outside and listen. It was a hot night, and the schoolhouse wasn't air conditioned. Gathered outside in the yard were as many people as were inside, all listening to the show. "That was our first stage show," said Charlie, and the brothers were impressed with what they heard—and with the crowd. "But we knew at that point, when we saw Acuff pass in his car that day, we knew that's what we wanted to do. It was just a matter of how to do it."

THE RADIO TWINS

The plans got off to a rocky start, and for a time it seemed that events were conspiring against the brothers. In 1938 the Loudermilk house burned to the ground, and the family lost almost everything. Then Ira decided to get married; he had fallen in love with Annie Lou Roberts, a local girl, and the pair were married while they were still in their teens. By 1940, when Ira was only seventeen, he found himself a father (of a daughter named Gail) and realized that he was going to have to find a better way to support his young family. For a short time he moved to Rome, Georgia, where he stayed with relatives and tried to make it as a Good Humor man, pushing an ice cream cart through the streets. Next he moved to Chattanooga, where he got a "real" job working at the Peerless Woolen Mills.

It was thirty-eight miles from Chattanooga to Henagar, but Ira came home on weekends. It was then that the boys could work on their music, trying out new songs and rehashing old ones, accepting invitations to local dances, parties, and church socials. Ira began begging his father to let Charlie move to Chattanooga so they could continue singing together. "I think Ira knew he didn't have much of a lead voice," recalls Charlie. "He couldn't do much on his own. But if he could get me with him—together we were pretty damn tough." Colonel finally relented; although he honestly felt he needed Charlie on the farm, he was about as fond of music as the boys, and he understood what they were trying to do.

Ira had learned about a big weekly amateur contest held every Friday night at the American Theater in Chattanooga. Any act that could win first place for three weeks in a row would get the grand prize—a regular fifteen-minute radio show on the local 250-watt station. Ira and Charlie entered and won the first week singing the novelty song "There's a Hole in the Bottom of the

Ira as a teenager

Sea." The second week they did "Johnson's Old Grey Mule," another novelty, and won again. The third time, they repeated "Hole in the Bottom of the Sea," and found themselves with their own radio show. It took about two months for the station, WDEF, to find sponsors, and while waiting, the brothers went "busking" in beer joints around Chattanooga. "We worked with a buck dancer named Jimmy Brown," Charlie recalls. "Back in those days, most bars had just a pool table, but no juke box. We would go in and sing a song and Jimmy would dance a number and then pass the hat. If there was anything in the hat, we'd sing another song. We'd keep doing this until nothing came back in the hat."

Finally, the show was set up, and Ira and Charlie went on the air under their first stage name, the Radio Twins. This was in late 1942. Their show was a fifteen-minute affair that went on the air at 4:30 in the morning, and although the station was only a 250-watter, it broadcast on a frequency that was reasonably clear. The boys soon began getting mail from as far as a hundred miles away and found that even their friends and family on Sand Mountain could pick them up. They began to get show dates as a result of the broadcast, their first engagement being a concert in Jasper, Alabama, in the courtroom of the county courthouse. They soon fell into a demanding routine as they tried to balance their radio work, their day jobs at the cotton mill, and their personal appearances. Charlie lived with Ira and his wife, and their day started early. "We'd get up at three, have coffee, go do the early morning radio show. Then we'd come back, eat breakfast, and go to the mill and work all day long. Then leave the mill and go to some little place and work a show date. You got back at twelve or one or sometimes even two in the morning, sleep a few hours, get up at three again to start all over." They were finding out fast just how hard it was to break into the still-new country music profession.

The show only lasted a few months, and then Ira got his draft notice. This was 1943, and World War II demanded mobilization all over the country. Ira reported to Fort Bliss for basic training, and Charlie returned to the farm on Sand Mountain. It appeared that their career would be put on hold again. Then, during a basic training exercise, Ira hurt his back. After army doctors examined him, they decided to discharge him; after eighty-nine days, Ira was back home. The brothers immediately returned to Chattanooga to resume their career. Their radio show was history, but neither of the young men was too worried about it; it was a lot of hassle, and not much had come of it. Off and on they had been talking with Bob Douglas, a local radio star and fiddle player, about working with him. Douglas had seen the pair win at the American Theater talent show and had been impressed with them then, and wanted to offer them a job with his band. Douglas had been a fixture in the Chattanooga music scene since the 1920s; he had recorded with the Allen Brothers for Victor and had worked with artists like Pete Cassel, Curly Fox, and Clayton McMichen. He had a good show on the powerful 5,000-watt station WAPO, and a popular band called the Foggy Mountain Boys (some five years before Lester Flatt and Earl Scruggs appropriated the name).

Both Charlie and Bob Douglas date the brothers' becoming Foggy Mountain Boys to late 1943. Ira did some of the announcing for the show, and the broth-

Bob Douglas and the Chattanooga band, The Foggy Mountain Boys (Ira and Charlie on R)

ers sang the band's theme song, the old Carter Family favorite "Foggy Mountain Top." The band included bass player Charlie Bell, Douglas, Ira and Charlie, and a comic named Uncle Ben. Douglas was a superb fiddler and could back the brothers on the older sentimental songs that they now started featuring. Home recordings from the period have survived and show Ira and Charlie doing pieces like "Dust on the Bible," "Take the News to Mother," and "You Cast Me Out." Their young voices sound more like the Blue Sky Boys than anything else; the sky-high harmony is not there yet, and the precision is not perfect yet, but the home discs do show why the early morning fans began to perk up at the brothers' music. (Two of these cuts are available on a retrospective of Douglas's music, *Sequatchie Valley* [Tennessee Folklore Society TFS 109].)

Throughout 1944 and into 1945, Ira and Charlie continued to work with the Foggy Mountain Boys, perfecting their music, making contacts, working school-houses and early morning radio. "Chattanooga, per capita, was the best country music town in the United States," Charlie says. Located at the junction of three of the most fertile country music states—Tennessee, Alabama, and Georgia—the town was a favorite venue for dozens of major singers. It was also a center for gospel music: the eastern branch office of the Stamps-Baxter company was there, and the hills around the town were full of singing conventions, shape note singers, and gospel quartets. Ira also began experimenting with writing his own songs for the act. One of the first of these songs was "Weapon of Prayer," which came out as the war was winding down, though it would not be recorded for years.

In July 1945, Charlie turned eighteen and immediately became subject to the draft. Since it was impossible for him to get a day job with certain induction hanging over his head, he went ahead and enlisted in the army. Soon he was stationed at Lowery Army Air Force Base in Denver. Ira wasn't interested in returning to the farm, though, and took his family to Knoxville. There he got

Charlie in uniform,
1945

a job as a fry cook in a local hotel and began to hang around the Knoxville radio stations. WNOX was especially alive at this time; Lowell Blanchard's "Mid-Day-Merry-Go-Round" had helped serve as a training ground for Roy Acuff and other Opry stars and was one of the best-known barn dance shows in the South. In the mid-1940s it featured people like Homer and Jethro, Bill and Cliff Carlisle, Archie Campbell, Chet Atkins, and Charlie Monroe. A local grocer named Cas Walker sponsored all sorts of country radio shows and concerts, making himself a nationwide reputation and earning the respect of dozens of young entertainers. The hills around Knoxville provided dozens of little towns and country schoolhouses where the musicians could "book out" and play concerts off their radio broadcasts.

Ira eventually got a job with Charlie Monroe and his Kentucky Partners. Monroe still had a major record contract with Victor and was known for his good gospel style as well as his willingness to use younger musicians and even electric guitars. His approach was more "country" than bluegrass, and thousands of fans found his music more accessible than the kind Bill Monroe played on the Opry. The Monroe Brothers had been among Ira's heroes when he was growing up, and he was delighted to be able to play mandolin with one of them. He also sang in Charlie Monroe's gospel quartets. Since the band already had a tenor, Ira—one of the music's greatest natural tenors—found himself singing bass.

Years later Charlie Monroe recalled his time with Ira. He remembered that Ira had talked about how important the Monroe Brothers had been to the Louvins as kids and how the Monroe Brothers' recording of "What Is a Home without Love" had been their father's favorite song. "Ira worked for me, and Charlie offered to work for nothing if I'd just take him along. I said, 'Charlie, that wouldn't be fair to you.' I said, 'Why don't you fellows just go like this 'til you get on your feet, however you want to,' and I says, 'if I can help you anywhere, I'll be glad to.' We took old Ira Louvin to Chicago to record, I did. RCA Victor. They charged us twelve dollars for a [hotel] room. Four boys in it at that time. And them crazy boys told Ira, said, 'Each of us is gonna have to pay twelve dollars!' Ira sat up all night! Wouldn't go to bed! Mad as a hornet! He was so sure it was going to happen."

Once Ira calmed down, he got a chance to make his first commercial recordings. On March 27, 1947, the band recorded four sides at the RCA studios. Charlie Monroe, of course, sang lead and played guitar; James Martin played fiddle; Ray Lambert played bass; Larry Iseley played electric guitar; and Ira played mandolin. The sides included "Down in the Willow Garden," "It's Only a

Phonograph Record," "I'm Coming Back but I Don't Know When," and "Bringing in the Georgia Mail." Some of them became classics of sorts. "Willow Garden," a version of an old English ballad, was copied by pop singer Art Garfunkel in the 1970s. "Georgia Mail," taken at a blistering breakneck tempo, spotlighted Ira's mandolin and showed just how well he could emulate Bill Monroe. In fact, he did such a good job that later listeners—including some RCA producers— mistook the recording for a Monroe Brothers original. Curiously, "Georgia Mail" was a song penned by a man named Fred Rose, a man who soon played a key part in the career of Ira and Charlie.

It was about this time, too, that the Loudermilk name got changed to Louvin. Even before Charlie went into the service, the brothers had talked about chang- ing it. "People tended to have trouble with *Loudermilk*," Charlie said. "They pro- nounced it wrong, spelled it wrong, sometimes even laughed at it. We wanted a name that was easier to spell. So we took the first three letters of *Loudermilk* and added the *-vin* to it. I'm not sure where we got the *-vin* from. Our sister used to say that one of our relatives had Louvin as a middle name, but we never could confirm that. We first used the name professionally in Knoxville, after I got out of the army. Even then we had trouble with people not pronouncing it right. Disc jockeys in Florida always used to call it LouVINE. We didn't get it legally changed in the court records until 1960, even though Fred Rose had suggested this earlier. My first two children were legally named Loudermilk, but my last one was legally named Louvin." In fact, on the union sheets for the Charlie Monroe session, Ira signed his name as "Ira Louvin Loudermilk" and gave his address as 534 East Fifth Street, Knoxville.

After Charlie returned from the army, Ira quit his job with Charlie Monroe and the pair at once resumed their career. For a time, they tried using the name "The Sand Mountain Playboys," but this name didn't exactly fit with the kind of gospel and sentimental songs they were featuring. Finally they made the switch to "The Louvin Brothers" and began broadcasting and booking out with people like Bill and Cliff Carlisle. They first worked for Cas Walker at WROL; he teamed them with Willie Brewster and Hoke Jenkins, who ran a tent show and toured. After Ira and Charlie found out that the two "stars" were not passing on the money Cas Walker was giving them the brothers protested and soon found themselves out of a job again. Next they talked to Lowell Blanchard at WNOX, who paired them with the Johnson Brothers, Hack and Clyde, local favorites, and created a new gospel quartet. They were given a 5:30 AM show on WNOX, and played what bookings they could scare up.

"We were getting pretty close to starving to death, but not completely yet," recalled Charlie.

Then one morning in the spring of 1947 the brothers were having their corn flakes in a cafe across from the WNOX studios when a big man with a white hat came over to their table. "He looked like he just stepped out of a magazine," said Charlie. "It was Smilin' Eddie Hill." Although he is best remembered today as an influential early disc jockey—he is a member of the country disc jockey's Hall of Fame—Eddie Hill was a skilled entertainer and promoter who was to have a profound influence of the career of the Louvins. He was born in 1923 in the Polk County hamlet of Delano in the extreme southeastern corner of Tennessee. He attended Polk County High School in Benton, the nearest large town, and took an early interest in drama; in the sixth grade he had astounded his classmates by memorizing a part in a school play that ran to "446 tablet pages written in longhand." As a teenager, he was more a singer and a clown than a serious musician; once, at a rural show, Eddie and his band took the stage only to be met by a local policeman. The officer was there to repossess Eddie's guitar, on which he had missed some payments; "we talked him into letting us go on with the show and turn over what we took in to him," Eddie said. "Luck was riding with us because we took in enough to pay for it." On another occasion, Eddie and his friends found themselves stranded and penniless in downtown Chattanooga. Eddie noticed a poster advertising a talent show at WDOD with a first prize of fifteen silver dollars; he bluffed his way in, borrowed a guitar, and sang, danced, and clowned his way to first prize. By the time he left home to go to Knoxville (to get work in a cotton mill where his father was foreman) he was on his way to becoming a master showman. As soon as he could afford it, he bought himself the appropriate garb: "a new green suit, yaller tie, and yaller socks."

Hill's father was a decent old-time fiddler, and his grandfather played banjo. In spite of his front-man personality, Eddie quickly developed into a solid rhythm guitar player and got a job on the "Mid-Day-Merry-Go-Round" playing bass. In the summer of 1943, the team of Johnnie and Jack was broken up when Jack Anglin was drafted. Johnnie Wright recruited Eddie to replace Jack, and the band began working over WNOX, augmented by Johnny's wife Kitty Wells and the young Chet Atkins, who was then playing fiddle. Eddie stayed with the band until 1945. As he had traveled around with Johnnie and Kitty, he had heard the Louvins on their early morning show and had been impressed with their duet work. As Charlie recalls, "Eddie said he had sold a show to a radio station in Memphis. He had said, 'Would you buy this show if I had the country's best duet and the world's best band?' Of course, he didn't have any of this put together yet, but he had sold them on it. So now he was putting his band together, and came to see us." Determined to impress the boys, Eddie ordered them huge helpings of country ham and eggs and began talking. "Come to find out later," said Charlie, "that he had a borrowed diamond ring on, and a suit he had borrowed from Jack Anglin, and had borrowed the fiddle player's car to drive up to see us." But Eddie did a good sell; he was hiring some musicians away from Johnnie and Jack's band, and he wanted the Louvins too. The boys talked it over and agreed on the terms. A week later Eddie sent them a pair of Continental Trailways bus tickets to Memphis, and they took off.

THE LONESOME VALLEY TRIO

The brothers spent the next four years, from September 1946 until 1950, in Memphis; most of that time they worked with Eddie Hill. It was to be one of their longest stays in any one place, and it marked crucial transition time for them. During this Memphis tenure, they would make their first nationally distributed commercial records, publish their first songs, and perfect their unqiue harmony style. Hill's deal was with WMPS, and the brothers found themselves doing three shows a day with him. One was a twelve o'clock affair called "High Noon Round-Up," which featured the whole Eddie Hill band; for a time it included guitarist and mandolin player Paul Buskirk (later to perform with Willie Nelson, among others), Bill Ross on steel guitar, Tony Cianciola on accordion, John Gallagher on bass, and Harold Horner on piano. (This group made a handful of recordings for Apollo in 1949, at the same session in which Ira and Charlie cut their first side.) Then the Louvins and Eddie Hill had a separate daily show in which they called themselves the Lonesome Valley Trio and did primarily gospel songs. There was also the usual early morning show, at 5:30, Charlie recalls, "on which we'd sing one country song and a hymn." On top of that were constant personal appearances. "We did three radio shows a day and a stage show every night, seven days a week," recalls Charlie. "At first, we made twenty dollars a week, apiece, for this. We worked all over Arkansas, Mississippi, southern Missouri, and all of Tennessee. We did quite well—but a lot better for Eddie Hill than for the Louvin Brothers."

Hill had lots of irons in the fire; after the one o'clock Lonesome Valley Trio show, he had his own disc jockey show. For many of the personal appearances, the band had to leave as early as one o'clock in the afternoon even to get there, and often Eddie told the boys to go on ahead and get set up, that he would follow. But, Charlie recalls, "in the years we worked with Eddie, we

Ira and Charlie at Memphis, shortly after their first releases on Capitol

probably worked four hundred or five hundred dates where he never even did show up." But the popularity of the Louvins and the quality of Hill's band allowed him to get away with it. "He did have a classic band," says Charlie, one able to do everything from comedy to western swing. "We sang all kinds of songs. We didn't just sing gospel there. We did silly songs like 'Hole in the Bottom of the Sea' and songs like 'Knoxville Girl' and 'I'll Be All Smiles Tonight.' And we did true gospel songs, the church hymnal type sometimes, and then a lot of the new ones that we wrote, like 'I'll Live with God to Die No More.'"

It soon became obvious, though, that the Louvins' audience was more in-terested in their gospel songs. "Ira and I would get six thousand letters a week from people requesting hymns," Charlie remembered. The brothers also began to explore—when they had the time—the idea of doing shows in churches. This bothered them a little. Ira had always been told he should have been a preacher, and always felt guilty about not "taking up his calling." He resisted the tempta-tion to preach to audiences when the brothers were on stage, but he did start creating songs like "Satan Lied to Me," which had a middle section that was a recitation—a recitation that sounded a lot like a mini-sermon. Another question was whether they should accept pay for singing at churches. This problem usually was solved by letting the local preacher take up a "love offering" from the audience and turn this money over to the singers. Once Eddie Hill went with the Louvins to a country church singing and was amazed to see that they got a love offering of over two hundred dollars. It was all the Louvins could do to hold Eddie back from a sudden plan to take their show into churches every night and reap a fortune in love offerings.

Ira and Annie Lou, meantime, had been having troubles. They had some serious fights even before the group left Knoxville, and now, after a short time in Memphis, she took their daughter Gail and returned to Sand Mountain. Soon after that the couple divorced. Charlie, for his part, had met a young woman named Betty Harrison from Meridian, Mississippi. "I met her in a Wal-green's drugstore in Memphis," Charlie recalled. "She gave me a free dinner, and that impressed me." Meridian was the birthplace of Jimmie Rodgers, and Betty could remember that when she was a baby, Rodgers had met her family and even bounced her on his knee. There was a courtship, and Charlie and Betty were married in an informal ceremony in Hernando, Mississippi, on Septem-ber 18, 1949.

Memphis in the late 1940s was an exciting crucible for country music. The Delmore Brothers and Wayne Raney were on the radio and were touring the

same circuit as the Louvins, exciting fans with their new country boogie. Slim
Rhodes and his Southerners were merging western swing with country. Curly
Williams, a Columbia star who had written songs for Hank Williams, worked
out from Memphis radio. The leading disc jockey on WMPS was Bob Neal, who
later played a role in the career of Elvis Presley. It was about this time, too, that
the gospel-singing Blackwood Brothers decided to make Memphis their base,
opening up another type of music. It is hard to know just how much impact
the Louvins might have had on the younger singers in the area; did young Elvis
Presley, for instance, tune into the early morning Eddie Hill show, or the 1:00
PM gospel songs of the Lonesome Valley Trio? One youngster who did hear
and learn from them was Johnny Cash: in his autobiography, Cash mentions
that he listened faithfully to the brothers and came to see them in person
when they played in Dyess, Arkansas. Charlie Louvin, Cash recalls, walked
right up to him and asked where the rest room was. Awestruck, the young
Cash escorted Charlie there and then waited outside to escort him back to
the stage.

Ira and Charlie with Johnny Cash,
ca. 1957

It was during these years that the brothers got serious about writing songs. Charlie thinks the first time they ever tried to write a song was in 1941. They came up with a good lyric but were not confident that they could add a melody to it. After struggling awhile, they finally saw a magazine ad offering to have "professional" tunesmiths put a melody to their lyric. "It was one of those deals where they write you back and say your words are good, and for an extra twenty-five dollars they'll help out more, and do this and do that. When they sent it back, we got somebody to play it on the piano, and we didn't like the tune they put to it. So that was a lesson learned." There wasn't much further attempt at songwriting until around 1945. By then, Ira had emerged as the songwriter in the duo, and throughout their career he produced the first drafts of most of the Louvin songs. One of his earliest efforts was "Alabama," which dates from 1946 and which the brothers recorded several times. But the Memphis years saw a veritable explosion of creativity from Ira; once he began, he produced dozens of originals, from gospels to novelties. The brothers often tried the new numbers out on their radio show, and Eddie Hill found himself singing many of them and liking them.

Charlie recalls: "When we went to Memphis, we had never had a song published. Like it still is now, if you didn't know somebody, you couldn't get in to see anybody. You had to go in and get introduced to a big shot in order to even have anybody listen. So Eddie said, 'Well I know a publisher, and I believe I can get these songs published.' We must have given him twenty-five songs to take with him the next time he went to Nashville." Hill did have good Nashville connections, and one of them was Fred Rose, who was running Acuff-Rose publishing company. One of the most astute song judges in music history, Rose looked over the Louvin songs and listened to wire recordings that the brothers had made as demos. He liked what he heard, bought the songs, and decided to sign the Louvins to an exclusive writing contract. It was the start of an association between the Louvins and Acuff-Rose that extended throughout the brothers' career.

It was only later that the brothers learned that Hill had added his name to most of the songs, cutting himself in for a third of any royalties. This was not all that unusual in those days—artists routinely insisted on becoming "co-authors" when they cut a song—and Hill may have felt that his name recognition helped get the songs placed. The Louvins didn't see it that way, though. Some of the songs included what would later become Louvin standards: "God Bless Her Cause She's My Mother," "Robe of White," "I'll Live with God (to Die No

More)," and "No One to Sing for Me." Others were less well known but interesting; many were never even recorded by the brothers themselves. There was "Bless Your Little Thumping Gizzard," "Are You Afraid to Die," "A Hard Road to Travel," "Little Mary," "My Heart Was Trampled on the Street," "Whispering Now," and "Tiny Broken Heart."

Word about the new songwriters spread fast in Nashville, and Fred Rose helped the brothers get "cuts" of several songs on records by major artists of the day. Probably the first non-Louvin group to record a Louvin song was a duo called Mel and Stan, the Kentucky Twins; they did a "hillbilly sacred vocal" of "Whispering Now" for Capitol in May 1949. A few months later Red Sovine recorded "A Hard Road to Travel" on the MGM label, and Ira's former boss Charlie Monroe followed with "Gonna Shake Hands with Mother Over There" for RCA in March 1950. During the next few years groups like Johnny and Jack, Jim and Jesse, and Carl Smith all cut Louvin songs. And some had considerable success. "I'm Gonna Love You One More Time" got a lot of airplay for Johnnie and Jack, and "Are You Missing Me" became one of the best-known of Jim and Jesse's Capitol sides. Carl Smith, whom the Louvins knew at WROL in Knoxville, may have had the first chart hit with a Louvin song with "Are You Teasing Me," recorded for Columbia in May 1952. Two groups, Carl Story's bluegrass band on Mercury and Bill Carlisle's band the Carlisles, seemed almost to specialize in Louvin songs. Story preferred the early gospel efforts like "God Saved My Soul," while Bill Carlisle was drawn to novelties like "Is Zat You Myrtle?" (which actually charted in 1953) and "Shake a Leg." Roy Acuff, whose show had inspired the brothers a generation earlier, did "Baldknob, Arkansas" at his last Columbia session in 1951 and later cut "Little Mary" for Hickory. Wilma Lee and Stoney Cooper recorded the Louvins' "West Virginia Polka" for Columbia in July 1951. In fact, during their first few years with Acuff-Rose, the brothers saw more of their songs recorded by others than they were able to record themselves, and they probably made more money from their songs than from their singing at this time. It was beginning to look like the Louvins would have a career as behind-the-scenes songwriters rather than performers.

Finally, however, they were able to begin their own recording career. Their first commercial side had been cut in 1947, with a band put together by Eddie Hill, for the independent Apollo label. The session was actually scheduled under Hill's name and held in Nashville. Apollo was a New York label started by Bess Berman and geared to jazz, gospel, calypso, Yiddish music and comedy. Their spectacular success with gospel great Mahalia Jackson had given them a national standing, and now they were tentatively exploring the country market. They had signed Hill, Johnnie and Jack, and a handful of others. The sessions took place in what is generally considered Nashville's first real recording studio, the Castle studio in the old Tulane Hotel on Church Street in downtown Nashville. The studio had been started by engineers from WSM radio who were moonlighting for the increasing number of record companies that wanted to record in Nashville. The Louvins were in the studio for all four of the sides recorded by the Hill band, although they actually sang only on "Alabama." "We got our names on the record," mused Charlie. "It was over on the side, in letters almost as big as the copyright notice: 'Vocal Refrain by the Louvin Brothers.'"

The brothers had been singing "Alabama" for some time before it was recorded. "It was written about 1946," says Charlie. "Basically, Ira wrote the song to explain how we were raised. To explain the countryside that we lived in. The song later on was cut several times, and it never was a big single, but a lot of people liked it. It explains the dogs and the roads and the mountains and the flowers and a lot of things about the state." Charlie felt that Eddie Hill had contacts in Nashville, especially with Decca boss Paul Cohen, and that Cohen actually might have helped them get the Apollo session. Whatever the case, the backup band included Hill on rhythm guitar, Tommy Jackson (another superb musician who was to become the leading session fiddler in Nashville in the 1950s), Lightning Chance on bass, and the Louvins on mandolin and guitar. When the record was released, the flip side was a piece called "Melting Steel" that featured Hill's steel guitar player, Billy Ross, from Tingall, Georgia. "There's no telling how much the record helped us," recalls Charlie, but copies of it were pretty rare, suggesting that actual sales were not great.

Better luck came when their publisher Fred Rose used his connections in Nashville to get the Louvin sound, in addition to the Louvin songs, on record. In the late summer of 1949 Rose managed to get the Louvins "half a session" with Decca. "Half a session" was half of a standard three-hour studio session; in those days, a full session was good for four songs. In this case, the Louvins were allowed to cut two masters while another artist (one named Bob Price) used the other half of the time to cut two masters. Part of Rose's plan was to get more attention for two of what he considered the Louvins' best and most commercially viable songs. He was nervous that the Decca A & R (Artists and Repertoire) men would try to force "unsuitable" songs on the duo, but as it turned out, they wound up cutting two of their best numbers, "Alabama" and "Seven Year Blues."

Ira and Charlie receiving another award from their old friend Eddie Hill

The Decca bosses were not at all worried that the brothers had already recorded "Alabama"; Apollo was such a "small" label that it presented no real challenge to the market. The Decca officials also knew that some seven months earlier RCA had cut a version of "Alabama" by The Blue Sky Boys—the boyhood idols of the Louvins. That record had just been released a few weeks before the Decca session, which was on August 23, 1949. "Seven Year Blues," which would later be recorded by bluegrass patriarch Bill Monroe in 1960, was also to become a Louvin standard.

The main thing Charlie remembers about the Decca session—which was the only such one for the Louvins—was its brevity.

We cut that session in eight or nine minutes. We'd waited out in the hall [of the Tulane Hotel]. Lonzo and Oscar [an Opry comedy duo] were in there recording and having all kinds of problems getting their song all together. And we went in, after waiting until three o'clock in the morning for the studio. Went in and started the session and went straight through it. We were cutting from a microphone straight onto a disc. The first one we cut, they accepted. Of course, I'm not saying it couldn't have been better. But we cut it on the first take, then went on and did the same thing for "Seven Year Blues." Ira and I had been singing it so much we knew it forwards and backwards and sideways. Usually if the artist knows his material, you don't have much of a problem out of the band.

In this case the band was a mixture of the regular Eddie Hill band and Nashville studio men; among the former were steel guitarist Don Davis, accordion player Anthony Cianciola, and mandolin player Paul Buskirk. The studio men included bassist Lightning Chance and fiddler Dale Potter. Decca issued the single in October 1949.

During all this time, Ira continued to produce songs for Fred Rose to look at. Rose was riding the crest of the greatest country music phenomenon in history, Hank Williams, and this made Rose the most powerful man in country music. Everybody listened to him and heeded his genius with finding and editing songs. Charlie recalls that Ira could toss off songs at the drop of a hat, but that he didn't respond too well to criticism. "He'd ask me if I liked a new song he was working on," Charlie recalls. "And if I had any little reservation about it, he'd be likely to just crumple it up and throw it away." When Fred Rose approached Ira about editing or improving one of his songs—as Rose did with Hank Williams and dozens of other writers—Ira would reject the offer and say, "Fred, if you don't like it, I'll just write another one."

Nervous about trusting Eddie Hill with any more songs, and painfully aware that neither brother could really read or write music well enough to make out a lead sheet, the Louvins worked out a system to present their songs directly to Fred Rose. Once they had actually signed on as exclusive writers for the company, around September 1948, they would call Fred when they had a day off. As Charlie remembers:

If we found out we weren't working on, say, a Sunday, we'd call Fred and tell him, "This Sunday is the only date we've got open for the next three months and could we come up to Nashville that day." We'd go to his house, not the office; he had a little studio out back there where he was set up to cut demos. We'd drive into Nashville from wherever we were, over in west Tennessee or Memphis or Arkansas, and we'd try to get there at eight o'clock in the morning. That was about the time Fred got up. If we mistimed it and got into town a little earlier than that, why we'd just eat breakfast to kill time before he got up. A lot of times we'd get in there just shot—no sleep, no rest, driving half the night. But we'd have fifteen or twenty songs to turn in. He'd turn the tape recorder on, and we'd sit there and sing the new songs for him. Then later he'd have them transcribed and would get his people to pitch them to other artists. They would never actually copyright or publish a song until they got notice from the record company that it had been recorded by somebody and was actually gonna be released.

By the end of 1949 the brothers were beginning to feel that they had "played out" the Memphis area. This was the problem that had always plagued the old radio singers, whose personal appearances were geared to the driving distance from the home station. There were only so many country schoolhouses and full gospel churches and lodge halls and auditoriums and small towns in an area, and you could only play them so often if you wanted to draw decent crowds. The Louvins had worked themselves up to sixty dollars a week with Eddie Hill, but they were working hard for it. In addition, they had gotten wind that Hill himself was planning a move—to WSM in Nashville. (As it turned out, he did not formally make the move until February 1952, but he became one of Nashville's best-known announcers and disc jockeys.) Then early in January 1950 came an offer for the Louvins to return to their former base of operations in Knoxville. Lowell Blanchard was offering them two hundred dollars a week to appear on his "Mid-Day Merry-Go-Round" and a newer show called "Tennessee Barn Dance." The Louvins liked the odds and decided to sign on.

SONGS THAT TELL A STORY

Their second Knoxville stay should have been a boost to the Louvins' career. Lowell Blanchard's shows had been acting as a sort of triple-A farm club for the Grand Ole Opry for some years, and the Louvins had been looking for ways to get their foot in the door there for months. Knoxville was a good town for the kind of older duet singing the Louvins did so well. Charlie Monroe had been there, as well as the Bailey Brothers, gospel greats Grady and Hazel Cole, and the Birchfield Brothers. Wally Fowler had developed the Oak Ridge Quartet, one of the more popular gospel acts, while working there.

The brothers continued to sing the kind of songs for which they were best known; a songbook they put together in 1950 contains favorites like "Are You Afraid to Die," "Childish Love," "Love and Wealth" (later to become a bluegrass standard), "Land of Eternal Peace," and "I'll Live with God to Die No More." But they also—probably with the encouragement of master showman Blanchard—began to expand into other areas. They added recitations—musical settings or songs that had spoken parts of poetry or inspirational speech—such as "I'm Not Afraid" and "I Am a Shut-In." (This was an age in which recitation was a major staple of country music, with the success of T. Texas Tyler's "The Deck of Cards" and Hank Williams's "The Funeral.") The brothers continued to do novelty songs, and the 1950 songbook contains "Hang Out the Front Door Key," a piece from the 1920s, and "Is Zat You Myrtle," which Ira wrote for fellow Knoxville singer Bill Carlisle. Ira began to do character comedy, inventing a personality named Sal Skinner; as "Sal," he would don a bonnet and old fashioned gingham dress, and do a manic Minnie Pearl routine. Often he appeared with a device called "The Hooten-Nannie," a washboard festooned with bells, cymbals, bicycle horns, a racoon tail, and a bizarre owl's head mask. It was a far cry from the intense, dynamic Ira of gospel songs.

The Louvins with "Sal Skinner," from "Financial Flats, Tennessee," a Minnie Pearl type character played by Ira (shown here in a trick photo)

Within a few months after their arrival in Knoxville, problems developed. Ira began to have trouble controlling his explosive temper. "He didn't like his mandolin going out of tune on him," remembers Charlie, "and he'd get furious about it, even throw it. One day he finished a song and threw his mandolin all the way across the stage. Lowell Blanchard was watching, and came up to us, and said, 'I'm gonna let this go for now. But if that ever happens again, you won't need to come and look me up, you can just consider yourselves fired.' Of course, I knew it would happen again, so we just went on right then and started looking for a new job."

Almost at once they got wind that WBIG in Greensboro, North Carolina, was planning to start a barn dance show. The Louvins were offered a spot if they could come up with a full string band to back them up. They did; and although neither brother liked to describe the band as a bluegrass band (Ira especially didn't like to be called a bluegrass musician, even though he loved and respected Bill Monroe's music) in many ways it resembled one. On banjo was Wiley Birchfield, a native of Bryson City, North Carolina, who had been playing at WNOX. The fiddler was Page Hepler, a twenty-eight-year-old native

of Lexington, North Carolina, who had been a fixture at area fiddling contests before his stint in the navy during World War II. "His favorite girls are
all blondes," read the caption about him in the Louvins' songbook. The band
was assembled just before the brothers left WNOX, and soon they were all on
the road to Greensboro, driving a new 1950 Nash Ambassador and full of high
hopes. The Louvins were able to bill themselves as Decca recording artists, and
once again things were looking up.

And, once again, frustration. WBIG never managed to get its barn dance
show off the ground, and after a couple of months the brothers were again
looking for a decent radio job. Glen Thompson of WDVA in Danville, Virginia,
offered them work on the "WDVA Barn Dance," so they broke up their band
and moved up to Danville. Their salary was fifty dollars a week, and as they
struggled to supplement it by booking out, Charlie's wife Betty was able to get
a day job and bring in some money. Ira, in the meantime, continued to court a
woman he had met in Knoxville, Bobbie Lowery, and before long they decided
to get married. The professional side of the brothers' lives, though, was going
from bad to worse. Airchecks (off the air recording) made during this time at
WDVA and preserved by the Country Music Foundation show the brothers still
being backed by a full string band and sounding as strong as ever. But neither of
them liked the idea of having to depend on Betty's job for eating money, and by
the end of 1950 they had decided to return to Memphis. "There was definitely
a slump in our finances," laughs Charlie. "So we decided to return to Memphis
and get day jobs and more or less quit the business." By December they were
back in Memphis, about where they had started out eleven months earlier. It
had been a strange year, and a long, discouraging odyssey.

Fred Rose was still happy with the songs Ira was writing for Acuff-Rose and
was still getting them recorded by his stable of singers, but he sensed that the
Louvins were personally frustrated with their career. Again he tried to help.
He had close ties with the new MGM label, the home of his most sensational
discovery, Hank Williams, and he now got the Louvins a new contract with that
label. Unlike the earlier one-shot deals, this was an agreement to do three sessions, or a dozen songs, over a period of months in 1951. MGM was happy to
have Rose even serve as producer. "We never met anyone from MGM," Charlie
recalls. "Because Fred did our recording in the Castle Studios in the Tulane Hotel." To back them on their first session, held on February 20, Rose assembled
a studio band from some of the best young session musicians in town. Tommy
Jackson, the fiddler who had backed everyone from Hank Williams to Rex Allen,

The 1950 Nash, with the Greensboro band

was there, as was a very young Chet Atkins to play lead guitar. Eddie Hill, who, in spite of his differences with the brothers still played the best rhythm guitar they had ever heard, came in as well.

The highlight of the session—one of the first two songs to be released and the only one to become anything like a hit—was "Weapon of Prayer." The Louvins had written it some years earlier. "It was at the tail end of World War II," recalls Charlie. "And the country was listening. You know, we only listen during, or right after, wars. When we were fortunate enough to get a vehicle to put it on (being MGM records), we recorded it. It did quite well. [The British guitarist and singer] Mark Knopfler's [1990] record did better, but the original did all right." It was popular enough that Acuff-Rose brought it out in sheet music. The brothers had been singing it on radio and at personal appearances for five years before they finally did the recording.

Backing the original issue of "Weapon of Prayer" was "They've Got the Church Outnumbered," a mildly paranoid anthem that reflected the fundamentalist-Pentecostal attitudes of many of the Louvin fans in west Tennessee. In a time of McCarthyism, UFO scares, and the renewed popularity of revivals, the song was right at home. It was also one of the first of Ira's gospel songs "with attitude"—

songs that reflected traditional values yet applied them to modern or topical themes. The other two songs done at this first full Louvin session were "The Get Acquainted Waltz" and "I'm Changing the Words of My Love Song for You," two secular songs. Regarding the former, Charlie recalls: "It's just however you approach a girl. And it was an attempt to get something off the waltz craze that was going around then." (It was a time of "The Shenandoah Waltz," "The Kentucky Waltz," "The Tennessee Waltz," and others.) While the two gospel sides were released in June 1951, Rose had trouble convincing MGM that the Louvins could also do secular material; the company shelved the other two sides until May 1952, when they finally brought them out. They remained the only non-gospel sides the Louvins recorded during their stay with MGM. Publications like *Billboard* studiously ignored all of the Louvins' early releases.

The second session, with personnel similar to the first, was held six months later on August 5, 1951, in Nashville. By now the first MGM record, "Weapon of Prayer," had been released and was doing well. By now, too, the Korean War was in full swing, and once again American families were getting letters telling them of death and tragedy. This may have been one reason MGM and Rose wanted the Louvins to put out "Robe of White," a song that had been inspired by World War II but that the brothers had written during the Korean War. Charlie says: "We just knew so many people that were in the war. I couldn't say just who the song was wrote about. I know that within three miles of our house [in Alabama], we had one family who lost four boys at Pearl Harbor. In one family—the Murdoch boys. That's probably the worst case that happened on our mountain." MGM rushed the single out by October, but rather little came of it.

The three other gospel songs from the session, though, formed a cross-section of the gospel styles that had influenced the brothers. On the refrain of "Do You Live What You Preach," one can hear the minor key of the old Sacred Harp singings. "I'll Live with God (to Die No More)" pays stylistic homage to the Monroe Brothers, with Ira doing an eerie imitation of Bill Monroe's high, soft tenor. The peppy, up-tempo "You'll Be Rewarded Over There" calls up the sound of the James and Martha Carson duets, which were the current rage on Capitol records. "I'll Live with God" and "Robe of White" were also among the songs Eddie Hill brought to Fred Rose back in 1947, ones to which he had added his name.

In spite of the string of MGM singles, the brothers continued to have doubts that there was any real place for an act based on old-time duet harmony in the country music world of 1951—a world of electric steel guitars, muted trumpets, and Crosby-like singing of Red Foley and Eddy Arnold. By the end of 1951 they were sure; Charlie remembers: "On the last day of 1951 we officially broke up the act." Ira went back to Knoxville, his wife's home town, and took a job as a grocery clerk with the Cas Walker stores. Charlie used the G.I. Bill to go to barber school, then got a job with the Memphis post office. This meant that both brothers were making a decent living, but it also meant that they weren't singing together. Fred Rose persuaded them to try one more session with MGM, and they got together in Nashville again on May 20, 1952, for yet another try. The result was their most powerful gospel statement to date.

"Great Atomic Power" was the most popular song from this session, one that became a staple and one that they would later rerecord. The idea for the song came from co-author Buddy Bain. "He was a sometime singer on the Eddie Hill show we were doing in Memphis," said Charlie. "He was born and raised in Corinth, Mississippi, and he'd drive down to Memphis once or twice a week to sing a song on the show. The song was his idea, something he came up with after they dropped the big one. Buddy was trying to write it and he wasn't too lucky in getting the song to say what he wanted it to say. Ira took his title and his notes he had and finished the song for him."

After the end of World War II, there had been a flurry of atomic bomb songs in country music, such as the Buchanan Brothers' "Atomic Power" (1946), "Old Man Atom" by the Sons of the Pioneers (1946), "There is a Power Greater Than Atomic" by Whitey and Hogan (1946), and "Jesus Hits Like an Atom Bomb" by Johnnie and Jack (1949). This fad had not yet ended when the Korean conflict renewed concerns about nuclear weapons and gave a new lease on life to the theme. Nevertheless, Charlie doesn't recall any of the composers of their song being especially aware of the other songs. "We were living in a very small world," he reflected.

About the second song from the session, "Insured Beyond the Grave," Charlie says: "My brother was a biblical scholar; a lot of people say he was called to preach. That's why he led such a miserable life, because he refused to accept the calling. That song is scripture; basically 'Insured Beyond the Grave' is directly out of the Bible. If somebody steals something, you've got insurance to cover it, but the Book says there's one thing you can't insure here is your soul."

While the first two songs were released back-to-back in July 1952 (probably because of the topicality of the atomic song), the latter two, "The Gospel Way" and "The Sons and Daughters of God," were held for release until January 1954, after the brothers had signed with Capitol (and after Charlie began his thirteen-month hitch in the army—a stint that led to a gap in the brothers' recording activities).

The brothers resumed their own show over radio station WMPS at 1:00 PM daily), and repeatedly auditioned for the Grand Ole Opry—but with no luck. Charlie recalls that during this time "we were both frustrated. We had auditioned at that point maybe eight times trying to get on the Opry. We didn't know anybody. We were confused. We didn't know whether to get out or stay in." The only bright spot, ironically, was Charlie's work as a mail clerk during days at the Memphis post office. "One day my postal supervisor said he could get Ira a job at the post office, making more money than Ira was in Knoxville. Ira had no phone then, and Betty and I got in the car and drove over there—about three hundred and fifty miles—and told Ira, and talked him and Bobbie into coming back to Memphis. He got on as a substitute mail clerk. I had passed my civil service exam, but he never did. The money was good anyway. That's when we started our show back up at WMPS, and we were singing again."

By now the brothers were finding themselves seen more and more as gospel singers. Their MGM records tended in that direction, and their radio show did as well. The surrealistic novelty and comedy songs Ira had been writing were giving way to more sober fare like "The Great Atomic Power" and "Insured Beyond the Grave." For a time, they traveled with a tent revival preacher on weekends, attracting crowds for the preacher and honing their own high, powerful harmony that was to become their hallmark. Acuff-Rose published their first fully commercial songbook in 1952, *Songs That Tell a Story*. The title did not especially refer to the old "story songs" or ballads that their mother used to sing, but something more modern. "Strange as it seems," they wrote in their earliest songbook, "most of our songs are written from true stories with which we are thoroughly familiar. In writing a song from a true story or poem, we believe you should have a clear picture of the subject if you expect it to be good. If you haven't tried it already you will find it is difficult to use your imagination entirely and make it sound real." Later that year, WMPS program director George Faulkner got the idea of doing a syndicated radio show with the Louvins; it too would be called "Songs That Tell a Story" and it would be something like the local radio show they did in the afternoon. Charlie says: "I had the feeling that Faulkner was trying to get somebody to finance it. He said, 'Let's make up several shows on tape, send a few out, and take the feelers we get off them and see if we can't get somebody to come in and do it right.'

Because Memphis was where the Garret Snuff variety show was syndicated out of, he felt we could get a similar thing going. He was a smart cookie, but the thing never did get going. He took a job and moved to Texas right after we got started, and the thing never got into mass production." The test market was to be on station WZOB in Ft. Payne, near Sand Mountain, and the brothers cut three weeks' worth of tapes in advance. As it turned out, that was the only market in which the show ever aired, and the whole project was soon abandoned. In a curious footnote to the story, Charlie years later found some of the tapes and allowed their release by the independent Rounder label. The original tapes had been set up to generate income through the new Acuff-Rose songbook, and the tapes Rounder used still had some of the commercials for the book in them. Once the Rounder LP came out, Charlie started getting songbook orders from the commercials. "Even today, there's never a week goes by that we don't get one or two orders with a dollar bill for this forty-year-old songbook."

ON CAPITOL

In spite of the fact that MGM had released five singles and that "Weapon of Prayer" had become a modest hit, both Fred Rose and the Louvins felt they were not being treated well at the company. Charlie likes to explain: "In the early 1950s, if you weren't Hank Williams or Patti Page, you had no business being on MGM, because that's where their bucks and time were spent." Rose decided the best bet might be to try Capitol. It too was a relatively new label—formed by pop songwriters Johnny Mercer and Buddy De Sylva and record store owner Glenn Wallachs in 1942—but it was unusual in that it was head-quartered on the West Coast. From the first it maintained a country division, but most of its hits had been generated by West Coast artists—people like Tex Ritter, Tennessee Ernie Ford, Tex Williams, Cliffie Stone, Jimmy Wakeley, and Merle Travis. For much of this time, Capitol's head of country had been Lee Gillette, but in the fall of 1950 he was replaced by one of his younger associates, Ken Nelson. It was Nelson who eventually signed the Louvins, and it was he who was to oversee the rest of their recording career. It was Nelson who, for better or worse, crafted the classic Louvin sound that won them their place in history.

Nelson was not a West Coast native but a Midwesterner and one of the few A & R men of his day who had actually worked as a musician. He began his radio career at age fourteen, as a pop singer, and later played banjo with a number of radio bands. By 1945 he was an announcer at WAAF in Chicago, was working as a plugger for a music publisher, and eventually was musical director for the well-known Chicago country music radio show "Suppertime Frolic." While there, he noted that one of his most popular acts was the veteran duo of Karl and Harty, close harmony singers from Kentucky who had created classics like "I'm Just Here to Get My Baby Out of Jail" and "Kentucky." By 1946 Nelson was also working as a local Capitol rep (one of his first acts was to sign Karl and Harty to Capitol), and in 1948 he was offered a full-time job as head of Capitol's lucrative radio transcription service. (Transcriptions were recordings made exclusively for radio play.) By 1950 he had replaced Gillette as head of the entire Capitol country division. Although Capitol's West Coast acts were still going strong, Nelson realized that the company would have to start thinking in broader terms—and start drawing from other regions, such as Louisiana, Texas, and, especially, Nashville. He began to make regular trips to Nashville to harvest the new young talent that was growing up in the shadow of Hank Williams.

It was Nelson whom Fred Rose called about the Louvins. "He got us on Capitol," recalls Charlie. "Fred Rose called Ken Nelson on the telephone and told him what he had. And he said, 'You need these guys.' Ken said, 'If you think I need them, well, send me a contract. Then you can record them until I get to Nashville.' So Fred was really the producer of those first two or three Capitol sessions, even though Nelson's name was listed as producer. I know he was there for the 'Family Who Prays' session." It was also Rose who scheduled the session, for September 30, 1952, in Nashville, at the Tulane Hotel, and it was Rose who lined up the session men. He built the band around the guitar work of young Chet Atkins, who had also played with the boys on MGM. At this early date, of course, Atkins was not known as the ace guitarist and producer that he would become in later years, but he was becoming well known among the musicians in Nashville. Charlie recalls why they liked Atkins. "His thumb style just seemed to lend itself." It also fooled a lot of country fans that the backup guitarist on these early sides was Merle Travis, since Atkins could sound uncannily like Travis when he wanted to.

The cornerstone of that first Capitol session was "The Family Who Prays," with Charlie singing lead and Ira joining in on tenor on the refrain. The title came from an old Loudermilk family saying; "this was burned in our mind like a brand is burned on an animal," remembers Charlie. "From the time we were old enough to know anything, we heard other people and our mother pray those beliefs. If you pray together, you'll stay together. We put it a little different: 'the family who prays will never be parted.' That could and truly does mean in the other world. We all know that we ain't gonna hold out long here. That's what the song was written about."

This song was paired (on Capitol single 2296) with "Let Us Travel, Travel On," a gospel song modeled on the old singing convention songs from the Vaughan and Stamps-Baxter books—another tribute to the boys' Sand Mountain

Ira and Charlie with their Capitol producer Ken Nelson

past. Together the two songs made up the first Louvin Brothers Capitol release, in late November 1952. The brothers didn't have to wait long for the results. "Three months after that record, Ken Nelson at Capitol sent us a check for $596. We didn't dare cash it until we had made sure it wasn't a big mistake. We called Ken and told him someone had made a mistake with the check, and he laughed and said, 'Haven't you heard of mechanical royalties?' We had never gotten a royalty check from MGM."

"Broad Minded" was the second Capitol release (Capitol 2381)—another "topical" gospel song about a new buzzword being heard for the first time in the early 1950s. "We should have gotten fired from Capitol Records," recollects Charlie. "That was our second release; it didn't sell nothing. Absolutely nothing. But they gave us another chance." It was backed by a song that later became popular with other gospel singers, "I Know What You're Talking About," a solo by Charlie.

Session 7 MARCH 23, 1953

I Love God's Way of Living (Ira & Charles Louvin)	Cap 2612
Born Again (Ira & Charles Louvin)	Cap 2510
Preach the Gospel (Ira & Charles Louvin)	Cap 2612
From Mother's Arms to Korea (Ira & Charles Louvin)	Cap 2510

The brothers soon found out that, even though they were doing secular songs on their shows and on the radio, they were not going to be allowed to record them. "Capitol had already hired Jim and Jesse as a secular duet, so they said, We'll give you a spot on Capitol if you want to be just straight gospel. We don't have one of them; we've got Martha Carson, but she's a girl and you all would be different. In the good days, they didn't duplicate. They didn't have six Faron Youngs on one label. . . . We would [have] loved to have sung some secular songs, as we had on MGM."

"Preach the Gospel" stemmed from the Louvins' second stay in Memphis, when they both wound up working for the post office. "That turned us loose, so we could sing on Saturdays and Sundays," says Charlie. Often during this time they worked with a Pentecostal preacher named Chuck Graves whose territory included Arkansas, Missouri, and west Tennessee. "We'd go into a town with this guy, town where they didn't have a Pentecostal church. We'd go in a tent. In ten days, at a ten-day revival there, we'd be there a couple of weekends. They'd take up enough money to buy enough lumber, enough free help, that they'd make it happen, actually have the church finished, and the last night of the ten-day revival would be done inside that brand new church house. I guess we were on more than a dozen of those. He'd preach in a community that did not have that denomination of a church, and that'd be his goal, he'd build one before he left there. And he never failed."

The Louvin songs doubtless helped attract the kind of crowds Graves needed for this effort. While they sang standards like "Nearer, My God, to Thee," they also sang their original songs and even wrote some for the occasion. "Preach the Gospel" was one of these. "That was one of their big themes, that you should preach the gospel. If you're gonna write about it, you needed a snappy tune, one that's quick and would lend itself to hand clapping. I think my brother wrote that because we had worked so many nights with this guy, and that was one of his strong speeches that he would give every night."

Charlie and Ira were both reared as Baptists and didn't agree with all the Pentecostal tenets, especially their ideas on dress. "They claimed if you dolled yourself up you were dressing for the devil. We sang a lot for [Graves] and enjoyed his company, but his true beliefs we didn't go with all the way." One idea they did agree with, though, was the one expressed in "Born Again." "I suppose Ira wrote that song from a true experience," says Charlie. "I feel like he really had that experience."

"From Mother's Arms to Korea," which uses the conventional imagery of gospel music ("from a foxhole to a mansion on high") as part of a topical war song, was derived from the death of a boy both the brothers had known on Sand Mountain. "I Love God's Way of Living," the first title recorded, is characterized by an early and odd echo effect on the last word of the refrain, "hell." (Some of the same effect was also used on "Born Again.") Charlie thinks this was the first session they did at which Ken Nelson was actually present, and it was probably Nelson who wanted to try this technical effect.

In April 1953, about a month after the second Capitol session, came another ugly surprise: Charlie was drafted. He was not happy about it. His wife was five months pregnant, the Korean War was starting to wind down, and Charlie felt that he had served his time in World War II. "I would have gone to Canada if I had known they were going to draft me again," he says. Sure enough, he wound up in Korea—as a mail clerk—and began writing to his various congressmen about his plight. (The loophole that had allowed Charlie to be re-drafted was the fact that his tour of duty in World War II had lasted only sixteen months rather than the usual twenty-four because of the overall demobilization at the end of the war. Thus he was still eligible for the Korean War draft.) Charlie wrote to his Tennessee senator, Estes Kefauver, and lobbied for a law that would require people like himself to serve only the number of months needed to make up their original two-year hitch. The idea found support, and a new law was passed. "The second it passed, they sent me a cablegram in Korea, with the bill number and everything in it. Three months later I was on my way home."

Session 8   SEPTEMBER 22, 1953

If We Forget God (Ira & Charles Louvin)	Cap 2852
Satan and the Saint (Ira & Charles Louvin)	Cap 2965
Satan Lied to Me (Ira & Charles Louvin)	Cap 2852
God Bless Her ('Cause She's My Mother) (Ira & Charles Louvin, Eddie Hill)	Cap 2753
Last Chance to Pray (Ira & Charles Louvin)	Cap EAP 1 825
No One to Sing for Me (Ira & Charles Louvin, Eddie Hill)	Cap 2753

Knowing that there was going to be an interruption of the Louvins' recording schedule once Charlie got overseas, and aware of the fact that the records were selling well, Ken Nelson had decided to stockpile some sides for future use. Charlie had been sent to Ft. Jackson, South Carolina, in the fall of 1953, and while there he was able to get occasional leaves; Nelson managed to set up some Nashville sessions. The first of these was in September and yielded six sides. Most of them would later show up on the famous *Family Who Prays* LP from 1958, but they were also issued as singles during 1954, when the brothers made no new recordings at all.

"If We Forget God" became perhaps the best known work from this session. Like so many of Ira's songs from this period, it is a rejection of modern styles or habits in favor of older, more traditional values. In this case, Ira applies the dictum not directly to morals per se, but to singing; he seems to criticize pop-styled gospel singers who are more interested in climbing "fame's golden hill" than in spreading a Christian message. Charlie still uses the song in his show today. "This is one of the songs I check people out on," he says. "When I hear someone say, 'I know a boy who can sing just like Ira, you can't tell 'em apart,' I say, 'Bring him over.' First thing I do, I put my capo on, hit an E chord, and say, 'Let's do that "If We Forget God."' I'll hit an E chord and he'll say, 'Oh, me and the boy I sing with, we do that in C.' I say, 'Well, Ira and I do it in E.' 'I can't take it that high.' So you don't sound like Ira Louvin if you don't do it in the same key. Takes the fire out of it. When you douse the fire in a song, you kill the song. Ain't nothing left."

"Satan and the Saint," with its odd shouted line at the start of each verse, is a sort of prelude to "Satan Lied to Me." The latter contains one of Ira's first recorded recitations, something at which he became increasingly adept. As we have seen, in the early 1950s such recitations were an important part of mainstream country. Artists who could do them well, artists such as Hank Williams, T. Texas Tyler, Red Foley, Stuart Hamblen, and Bob Atcher, were becoming role models for Ira. "He would never preach to an audience," says Charlie, "but he could get through the most sentimental recitation and never lose it, always keep a straight face." The recitation in "Satan Lied to Me" was based on a true incident that occurred at a rural Alabama church the brothers knew about.

"God Bless Her ('Cause She's My Mother)" gave the brothers a chance to pay homage to the Blue Sky Boys, with close, straight harmony all the way through. This is a song from their earlier Memphis period, and Charlie thinks it

THE LOUVIN BROTHERS

Album cover of Louvin
Brothers' best known
gospel songs

was actually based on an older "mother" song the boys had known since child-
hood. A similar "mother" song is "No One to Sing for Me," another early piece,
not to be confused with the popular gospel song "Who Will Sing for Me."

Session 9

Swing Low, Sweet Chariot (Traditional)	Cap 2965
Nearer, My God, to Thee (Lowell Mason)	Cap EA P2 825 (EP)
Make Him a Soldier (Charles & Ira Louvin)	Cap 3083
I Can't Say No (Charles & Ira Louvin)	Cap EA P2 825 (EP)

The second "stockpiling" session marked the first time the brothers recorded
music that was not original Louvin material. "Swing Low, Sweet Chariot" is
the old traditional spiritual, not the "Swing Down Chariot" version that was
then being popularized by the Blackwood Brothers and other gospel quartets.
It is taken at a surprisingly slow tempo, with an achingly high harmony by Ira.
"Nearer, My God, to Thee" dates from 1856, when composer Lowell Mason
set this music to an earlier 1841 text by Englishwoman Sarah F. Adams. It is
traditionally known as the hymn sung by the passengers on the sinking *Titanic*.
Charlie and Ira used it a lot while traveling with the Pentecostal preacher Chuck

Graves, and it is still in Charlie's repertoire totday. "Make Him a Soldier" is noteworthy for its use of "afterbeats," an "echo" or counterpoint technique popular with the old-time southern quartets the brothers had heard as kids.

During the thirteen months Charlie spent in his second tour of duty, he met young Jesse McReynolds, half of the famed bluegrass duo of Jim and Jesse. Like Charlie, McReynolds had seen his career interrupted by the draft just as the act was getting started. They got up a band to pick together while in Korea and called it the Dusty Road Boys. They also formed a close friendship. Ira, for his part, stayed in Memphis during this time, continued writing songs, and began a disc jockey show over WMPS, playing Louvin Brothers records and tapes. By 1954, Charlie had made it back home, and immediately went to reclaim his job at the post office. In the meantime, Ira had gotten the idea that there was good money to be made in Birmingham and wanted to try their luck on the radio down there. After all, they were natives of Alabama, and who better would understand their music than their own people? Charlie was dubious but agreed to go to his supervisor and see if he could get six months' leave to try Birmingham out. "I don't think so," the supervisor told Charlie. "I don't think much of you hillbilly singers anyway." Charlie then told him what he could do with his job, and the Louvins bought a 1953 Cadillac with the money saved from Betty's allotment check and took off south.

The Birmingham stay lasted from summer 1954 to January 1955 and was a disaster from the start. "When Ira said we could make a killing in Birmingham, I wanted to believe it," said Charlie. "I wanted to stay in the music business bad. Of course, if we'd been smart, we'd known better than that. You don't never do real good where you were born at. That's history." The sponsor of their show was a woman named Lady Benz, and the brothers got a hundred dollars for doing a thirty-minute show five days a week. They decided to hire a band, and the two band members took up most of the hundred dollars a week. Whatever the Louvins made, they would have to make on the road, doing personal appearances. At once they found that the market had been saturated by a local team named Rebe and Rabe, who for some years had been emulating the Louvin style. (Rebe was the uncle of current country singer Vern Gosdin.) Rebe and Rabe had recorded for the Tennessee label and won quite a following. Charlie remembers: "They had copied the Louvin Brothers style for years, ever since we first recorded. If they could get ahold of our record at nine o'clock in the morning, they'd put it on their noon show. So when we got down there, the people all thought we were impersonating Rebe and Rabe.

Our songs had been basically worn out in that country, so we couldn't do any good at all."

By the end of the year, the nest egg they had brought to Birmingham had vanished. Charlie had sold the mobile home he owned, the telephone had been taken out, and Charlie and his wife, their child, and Ira and his wife and child were all living in one half of a duplex: two bedrooms and a very crowded kitchen. "It caused a real problem," mused Charlie. "Not a fighting problem, but a what-are-we-gonna-do-about-and-how-can-we-survive-this sort of problem." No one ever mentioned that it was the worst move they had ever made. Ira consoled himself with writing songs and came up with one called "If I Stop Dreaming." But the radio show on WVOK was going downhill fast, and something had to be done. Money was running low.

WHEN I STOP DREAMING

Just Rehearsing (Charles and Ira Louvin)	Cap 3241
Love Thy Neighbor as Thyself (Charles and Ira Louvin)	Cap 3083
Where Will You Build? (Ira and Charles Louvin)	Cap 3467
Pray for Me (Ira and Charles Louvin)	Cap 3241

The next Capitol session generated four more gospel numbers, all designed to be released as singles. Throughout the early 1950s, gospel music and what the trade papers called "religioso" music experienced unprecedented popularity. It was one of the few periods in country or pop records in which gospel songs could be routinely released as singles and garner serious sales. It was an era about to end, but while it lasted it gave the Louvin Brothers the boost their music needed.

The backup band now included a man named Chester Reason on guitar. (Chet Atkins's RCA commitments were making it hard for him to do much free-lance work for other labels.) Reason was a capable guitarist whom Ira insisted on nicknaming "Ferno" (Fer No Reason). On piano was Marvin Hughes, who had emerged as Capitol's staff pianist for Nashville sessions. Later on, when Ken Nelson couldn't make sessions in Nashville, Hughes stepped in and substituted for him.

"Love Thy Neighbor" was the best-known song from this session; although it never got onto the country charts, it became one of the most requested numbers at the Brothers' personal appearances. It was used later that year in one of the Louvins' rare film appearances, done for Bill Gannaway in the Bradley studio in Nashville. The Gannaway films, originally shot on thirty-five-millimeter color film, have been used numerous times in various television syndication shows. As for the song, Charlie remembers: "It represents the absolute essence of how we were raised." The remaining two songs were "Pray for Me," another one of Ira's moving narrations, and "Just Rehearsing"; they were issued as Capitol 3241 in October 1955.

The only bright spot in their career was their Capitol recordings. They were selling well, and the brothers had established a good relationship with Ken Nelson, who had just approved their recording of "Love Thy Neighbor" and set up a session in Nashville for late January 1955. "We called Ken Nelson from Birmingham," reflects Charlie, "and told him we wanted to get on the Grand Ole Opry. We had auditioned before eight times without any luck. Ken told me he'd get back to us next week and let us know something about the Opry. I told him that we didn't have enough food to last us til next week, and we had to know something now. We had to give him a phone booth number and wait by the booth until he could call us back."

Nelson put a call into Jack Stapp at the Opry and tried a desperate bluff. "I've got a duet you need on the Opry," he began. "The Louvin Brothers. The Ozark Jubilee [the Springfield, Missouri, show that was then challenging the Opry for national attention] has offered them a job, but I told them I'd like to see them on the Opry. If you don't want them, though, I'll just go ahead and tell them to take the Jubilee job." Stapp took the bait. "Wait a minute," he said. "Maybe we can use them." Stapp set up a few details and then called the phone booth where Charlie and Ira were waiting. They were due in Nashville at the Opry office at 4:00 PM on Friday—three days away. The next day the wives and children went on ahead to Nashville, while Ira and Charlie wound up their affairs and started up Highway 11 to Nashville, stopping at Henagar on the way.

Charlie remembers vividly the details of the next few days. They got to Nashville early Friday morning, January 28, ate breakfast at Linebaugh's on lower Broadway, and walked around until early afternoon. They then went to the National Life building, just a couple of blocks from where they had made their first recordings at the Tulane Hotel, and met with Jack Stapp. He was pleasant enough, spoke to them for a while, and brought them in to Vito Pelleteri, the man in charge of music clearances and programming. "He told us what was expected of us," said Charlie, "and then said, 'Come on, I'll introduce you to the stage manager, Jim Denny.'" Ira and Charlie exchanged glances; Denny was the man for whom they had auditioned time and again in earlier years. He would listen to them sing their hearts out and, without comment, refuse them. It was only later that they found out that Denny had no authority at all to hire anyone for the Opry, that their auditions had been for the wrong man. Both resented this fact and began to feel that Denny's trick had actually prevented them from getting on the show five years earlier, as well as shaking their fragile self-confidence.

They entered Denny's office and took their seats. "We sat there ten minutes and were completely ignored," said Charlie. "Denny was looking at a paper on his desk. We were really getting the cold shoulder. Ira had the attitude that even if they throw us out, I'm gonna say this anyway. So he finally said, 'Well, Mr. Denny, we've got to go. We'll see you on the Friday Night Frolic,' which is what they called the Friday Night Opry in those days. And when he said that, Denny just acted like he was gonna lay his paper down, and looked up over his hornrims and said, 'Boys, you're in tall timber. You better shit and get it.' And Ira said, 'Well, we got the saws, you just show us where the woods are.' Of course, that was a sarcastic remark on Ira's side, and I'm sure that was the way Denny took it. He never did attempt to try to do much humane for the Louvin Brothers while we were there."

The point was, they were there. The first night on the Opry they did their new song, "Love Thy Neighbor," backed by the house band. "The house band was one we were familiar with, that had backed us on several of our records. Chet Atkins was still there, and Lightning Chance, the bass man. They called us back for an encore, and we did just another chorus. The Louvin Brothers were never hoggish, and the Opry was running on a pretty tight schedule then." After the show, the brothers went out into the alley back of the Ryman, greeted a crowd of well-wishers, and went down to Tootsie's to celebrate. The next day they started to look for a house.

Almost at once they ran into two problems. One was the need to find a good backup band so they could reap some advantages of the Opry association by doing some touring. The second was how to deal with their "all-gospel" image, and how to break out of it. The first problem was easier to solve than the second.

When they had been in Birmingham, they had hired guitarist Chester Reason. He played with a "rasp" that neither Chet nor other Louvin guitarists had, and both brothers liked his sound. The Louvins asked Chester to join them on the Opry (he had played on their Capitol session of January 29, when they had cut "Love Thy Neighbor") but he ran into trouble. "It was tragic about him," said Charlie. "His wife refused to move to Nashville from Birmingham. She finally got him to quit, and that started him drinking. He was playing in a bar down there and was on his way home one night and got killed in a car wreck. This was about six months after we joined the Opry."

Next they hired the guitarist whose sound was to enhance most of the great Louvin recordings for the next three years: Paul Yandell. A native of Mayfield in western Kentucky, Yandell had been auditioning for the Opry since he was seventeen; he had bought all of Chet Atkins's records and was adept at playing the "western Kentucky" style that Atkins, Merle Travis, Ike Everly, and Mose Rager had perfected over the years. Unsuccessful, he had gone to Detroit to get work. A friend, disc jockey Fonzie Davis, had booked the Louvins and learned they were looking for a regular guitarist. He told the brothers, "I know where there's a boy that if Chet Atkins has ever played it, he knows it. He knows all of your records, 'cause Chet was the player on them too. He's already got Chet's licks and everything down pat." Davis offered to bring Yandell down for an audition the next week and called him in Detroit to tell him to get on down to the next week's Opry. Yandell did go and auditioned for the brothers on Saturday night. Ira and Charlie were impressed, but so was Grandpa Jones; "I tried for years to get down here and nobody would pay me any attention," recalled Yandell. "Then two acts try to hire me." The next morning, the Louvins called Yandell early and wanted him to meet them in Prestonburg, Kentucky. "I played a date with them that night. This was in March 1955," says Yandell. His first recording session with the Louvins took place on October 29, 1955, the session that yielded "I Don't Believe You've Met My Baby" and "Childish Love."

Three other veteran musicians rounded out the new Louvin Opry band. One was George McCormick, a guitarist and singer who was one half of the Mercury duo of George and Earl and who had recorded earlier on his own. "George fronted and did some trio work with Ira and me on the road," said Charlie. "He was a good baritone singer." In later years, George became an Opry regular, often performing with Grandpa Jones. Then there were Smiley and Kitty Wilson, who did MC work and played bass, respectively. They were both natives of northern Alabama; Hamilton K. "Smiley" Wilson had recorded on a host of minor labels with such bands as the Rio Grande Rangers and the Circle 3 Ranch Gang, and had recorded songs like "Red Silk Stockings and Green Perfume." Mary K. "Kitty" Wilson had worked with the Moonlight Ramblers and had been on KWKH in Shreveport, Louisiana, before she met the Louvins. Although the pair was on WBRC-TV in Birmingham in 1952 and 1953, the Louvins met them in Gadsden, Alabama, and soon hired them to fill out their band. They left the band about the same time as Paul Yandell, and spent a while with Martha Carson. About 1958 or so Smiley took a turn managing and booking the Louvins.

Since Paul Yandell was the youngest and most inexperienced of the group, he soon became the butt of a host of practical jokes. A favorite prank was to offer him some Chicklets and replace the Chicklets with Feenamints, a powerful laxative. They would then send him out into an audience to sell songbooks, and watch as the Feenamints hit; at one point, Charlie recalls, "we had to cut him off those Chicklets because we thought he was gonna get too weak to stand on the stage." Another time Ira put Limburger cheese in Paul's guitar case and then accused him of not washing his socks. Yet another time Ira bought a pair of ladies' panties, put some ketchup on them, and put them in Paul's guitar case when he wasn't looking. "He'd open the case and put them right on top of the head of guitar," Charlie laughed. "The next day we'd be in a hurry; Paul opens his case to jerk his guitar out, and the 'bloody' panties would fall to the floor. There'd always be a roomful of people there. Paul never could figure out how those things got in his case." Other jokes were even more outrageous—and the stories of them less printable—but Yandell toughed it out and developed the Atkins-flavored guitar style to where it became an important part of the Louvin sound.

Ira and Yandell on a fishing trip

Although the Louvins sang a mixed bag of secular and gospel songs when they were in Birmingham, they were stereotyped at Capitol as gospel singers. And, to be sure, they still had a huge gospel audience, especially in some churches. "The Pentecostal churches and the Assembly churches, that's where the Louvin Brothers, especially the up-tempo tunes, that's where they lived," says Charlie. "There was one preacher, he got in the business, he would sit on the courthouse square and play Louvin Brothers music 'til he gathered a crowd, then he'd preach to them. We were always running into people who said that Louvin Brothers music caused them to live in a Christian home. I run into people constantly that make you feel like you're a preacher.... Because the songs don't mean that to the person who's singing them, using them commercially, singing them every day. You don't think about what they might inspire other people to do."

The early 1950s, though, began to see a change in how people perceived southern gospel music, a change that crystallized in part while Charlie was doing his second stint in the army. Groups like the John Daniel Quartet (on the Opry), the Blackwood Brothers (from Memphis), and the Statesmen (from Georgia) had made gospel music synonymous with the male quartet: four men and a piano. The success of Wally Fowler's All-Night Sings, the national publicity won by the Blackwood Brothers on Arthur Godfrey's television shows, and the spate of hit records by pop-influenced gospel singers like Jo Stafford and Gordon MacRae, had caused many fans to look down on "hillbilly" gospel singers. "We weren't accepted in the gospel field," remembers Charlie. "We sang gospel music, but we were carnival people as far as the quartets were concerned, because we played a musical instrument. They only used a piano in those days to sing gospel.... Merely because we played stringed instruments, that made them think of us as hillbillies, and they didn't want to be associated with that. But Louvin Brothers got so hot that they almost had to associate with us if they wanted to draw people. But it still didn't pay no money to speak of. Work a gospel show, make five hundred dollars; work a country show, make twenty-five hundred. We could have made a living in gospel music, but I guess we wanted to go beyond a living."

When they started on the Opry, the brothers were on the Prince Albert segment with Red Foley. "We were only allowed to sing one hymn on that portion because Foley always sang one hymn. The sponsor said two hymns was all they wanted; they were a tobacco company and said they couldn't sell tobacco with gospel music. So we had to change and starting mixing it up—we

Ira backstage at the Opry with Ralph Emery and Skeeter Davis, February 1961

had to do one gospel and one secular tune to get our equal representation on that part of the Opry." By early 1955 they had decided to talk Ken Nelson into letting them record some non-gospel songs for Capitol. He was reluctant; he told them about the case of Martha Carson, a well-established gospel singer on Capitol who had tried to make the jump to secular music. According to Charlie, Ken had told Martha and her manager, "If you're determined to try it, we'll try it. If it works, fine; if it doesn't work, that means your gospel fans are gonna drop you for doing it. And if it don't sell, you're off the label. It's that simple." They took the chance and lost, seemingly proving Nelson right. Now he made the same argument to the Louvins. "You know what you're gonna do on a gospel record, you know what's gonna happen with a gospel single, you got all those people who buy your records, and if you cut secular music, they might drop you just like they did Martha." The brothers agreed that Nelson had a stronger argument, but they were still faced every week with being on the NBC portion of the Opry and being allowed to do two secular numbers or one gospel and one secular number. "He felt we would fall on our face like

Martha had done," Charlie says. "But we didn't approach that end of the music like Martha did. She came on with a tune that was like 'Whole Lotta Shakin' Goin' On,' and her gospel people were really turned off by it. We weren't gonna make that much of a change."

Still, any change was a major gamble; things were starting to go really well, both on the Opry and on records, and a failure here could mean losing it all. As the next session approached, they looked through all the non-gospel songs they had written over the years and finally settled on one Ira had written a couple of years earlier, one that they had sung in Birmingham: a slow waltz called "When I Stop Dreaming." "We sang that song for a year, messing around with it," said Charlie. "We felt it was the bravest—that if we were gonna change with anything, we could get by with using that song. We had our part down pat. We rehearsed it religiously, and when we went into the studio, we cut it in only two takes." The session was on May 25, 1955, and for the first time, all four cuts were non-gospel material. Ken Nelson, in spite of his doubts, brought in a song himself, one from the catalog of Central Songs, a West Coast publishing company he partially owned. This song, called "Pitfall," took almost twenty takes to record and almost drove everybody crazy.

Session 11	MAY 25, 1955
When I Stop Dreaming (Ira and Charles Louvin)	Cap 3177
Pitfall (Smitty and Tennessee Smith)	Cap 3177
Alabama (Louvins-Eddie Hill)	Cap EAP2 769 (EP)
Memories and Tears (Jimmy Rule)	Cap EAP1 1106 (EP)

The real birth of the Louvin Brothers' country sound was "When I Stop Dreaming"; not only was it the first non-gospel song the duo did for Capitol, but it set the tone for the classic Louvin style that was to come. They were aware of what Ken Nelson had told Martha Carson when she had begged to record a non-gospel song: if the song failed, she would be off the label. It was not exactly encouraging for the Louvins, who were now asking to do the same thing. They anguished over what songs to record, knowing that their career might well be riding on this session. One possibility was "When I Stop Dreaming." Charlie believes Ira might have begun work on the song while Charlie was in Korea; then, during their desperate Birmingham days, they began singing it on the radio and at personal appearances. "We sang that song for a year, messing around with it. Everybody thought it was a good love song. At one time or another in life I believe we're all dreamers. Some of us dream all the time. And I believe the rest of the world would be a lot worse place, wasn't for us dreamers. We dream about it. The doers take it and do it and get rich off of it." They also liked the song as a waltz; "waltzes are twice as hard to sell, but if they get moving, they'll live a lot longer on the charts." All in all, it seemed a good bet for what they were trying to do. "We felt the bravest—if we were going to change with anything, we felt that we could get by with using that song."

The gamble paid off. The song was a success in the 1950s and has remained one ever since. Charlie estimates that it earned composer's royalties of some two thousand dollars a year for the next twenty years, and recalls that it has been recorded over a hundred times by people from Lonzo and Oscar to Ray Charles. The single by the Louvins became the first one released by Capitol after the brothers joined the Opry in January 1955; it was an auspicious debut. Released in July 1955, the record eventually climbed to number thirteen on the *Billboard* country charts—the first time a Louvin single had ever made them. Over the years, it became a country standard and a blue-chip stock. For once in their careers, the Louvins had made exactly the right move.

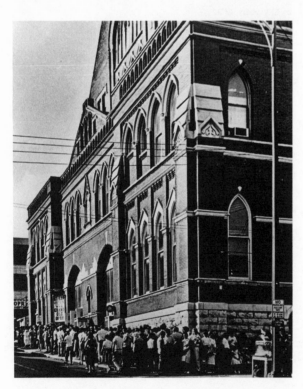

Nashville's Ryman Auditorium, home of the Opry when the Louvins joined in the 1950s

"Pitfall" was, except for a couple of old hymns, the first song the brothers recorded that they didn't write. It was penned by Smitty and Tennessee Smith, a radio duo whom the brothers had met in Atlanta. "The key to that is the publisher: Central," says Charlie. Central was a company that apparently was half owned by Ken Nelson (unofficially, because the Capitol bosses forbade their executives from owning music publishing companies). "When Ken owned half of the company he brought us lots of Central songs. Since, we felt, he had done so much for us, we felt obligated to pick and choose, and if there were any songs we could sing, we should sing them. And we did."

A similar motive was behind the recording of "Memories and Tears" by veteran songwriter Jimmy Rule, best known for being the co-author, with Hank Williams, of a book on how to write country songs. The brothers didn't know Rule personally, but they did know that songs by publishers like Cedarwood were important, especially if you wanted the advantages of Jim Denny's talent agency. Murray Nash, a longtime Acuff-Rose plugger and later Mercury director, brought "Memories and Tears" to the duo. Joe Lucas also watched out for good songs the brothers could sing, and he later brought them good material.

CASH ON THE BARRELHEAD

During the following two years (through 1955 until mid-1957), the Louvins found themselves with a string of hit singles, professional booking and management, and a national radio base from the stage of the Grand Ole Opry. While their careers continued to develop on a number of fronts and their personal

Live on Opry, ca. 1960

lives became increasingly complex, a crucial part of their legacy was being forged in the Nashville recording studios. Now Ken Nelson and the Capitol bosses couldn't seem to get enough Louvin recordings. In 1956 alone, they were in the studios almost every other month, eventually amassing some thirty-two sides. Many were still earmarked for singles, or for the increasingly popular 45 "EP" or extended play album—mini-albums that contained four songs, as well as a cardboard cover and even liner notes. Soon Nelson was urging them to begin thinking of yet another format—the LP album. During all of this activity, the pair continued to produce session after session and song after song that continued to define their music and style.

Session 12   OCTOBER 29, 1955

Don't Laugh (Rebe Gosdin)	Cap 3630
I Don't Believe You've Met My Baby (Autry Inman)	Cap 3300
Childish Love (Ira and Charles Louvin)	Cap 3413
In the Middle of Nowhere (Ira and Charles Louvin)	Cap 3300

In terms of sheer chart action, "I Don't Believe You've Met My Baby," by Autry Inman, was the Louvins' biggest hit, bigger even than "When I Stop Dreaming" at the time. It got to number five on the charts in January 1956 and stayed on the hit charts for an incredible twenty-four weeks—almost half a year. "That song came to us as a 'real life' song," says Charlie. "It wouldn't have sold that way. Ira asked Autry if it'd be all right if he added something to the song— not to get none of it, we didn't want none of the song. And Autry said, 'Well when you add what you add, let me hear it. And I'll tell you if I like it.' The song started off, 'Last night my dear the rain was falling, I went to bed so sad and blue, and then I had a dream of you.' That wasn't part of Autry Inman's lyrics at all. Ira took what he had tried to write as a real thing and turned it into a dream, made it sound like a dream, and it did go." In the original, then, the first verse as performed by the Louvins was totally missing. The song was originally published by Tree.

In a curious footnote to this account, Charlie recalls that by coincidence the flip side of "I Don't Believe You've Met My Baby" was a Louvins-Acuff-Rose song, "In the Middle of Nowhere." After the record became popular, Autry and the brothers compared royalty statements.

Autry would bring his statements that he would receive from Tree and he wanted to see our statements that we received from Acuff-Rose, 'cause he didn't feel like he was getting all his money. We showed him that the B side of the record made five times as much BMI as his A side did. There wasn't nothing he could do about it. In the old days, Acuff-Rose had four or five people on the road, and if, say, Steve was a disc jockey, and they came to Steve and they wined and dined him and treated him like a king, even if they had the B side of the record, they would get Steve to list the B side. "Go ahead and play the A side, we don't care what you play, but when you fill your reports out, put down our song." . . . And they did. Wesley [Rose] often said, "If there is a side, it'll be the Acuff-Rose song." By saying that, he meant he would kill the A side if it wasn't their song. If there was any way he could kill it, he would, by trying to make the B side of the record be the hit. They proved a lot of times they were strong enough to do that.

In spite of the fact that "Baby" was on the charts the longest, Charlie recalls that "it didn't sell half the records" that "When I Stop Dreaming" sold. One reason: "Because 'When I Stop Dreaming' was a waltz. If you can ever get a waltz to come alive, it'll live longer."

Although the brothers had gone up against the other Alabama duo of Rebe and Rabe earlier in their career, Rebe Gosdin's "Don't Laugh" did not stem from this encounter. As well as Charlie remembers it, the song was pitched to them by Ken Nelson. It was not issued until February 1957, when it showed up as the flip side of "The New Partner Waltz."

"Childish Love," Charlie thinks, was written about one of Ira's early wives. (He eventually had four.) "He was trying to tell her that she needed to grow up." The Louvin family and their community around Sand Mountain saw couples marry as early as age thirteen or fourteen. This song had been around for a while; it appeared in a 1950 songbook, dating from their years with Decca.

Session 13   MARCH 25, 1956

Hoping That You're Hoping (Betty E. Harrison)	Cap 3413
The First One to Love You (Helen Carter)	Cap 3715
I Cried after You Left (Faye Cunningham)	Cap 4941
That's All He's Asking of Me (Ira and Charles Louvin)	Cap 3467

"Hoping That You're Hoping" bore the composer credit "Betty E. Harrison," which was the maiden name of Charlie's wife. It was originally a Cedarwood song, listed under Betty's name to get around the Acuff-Rose contract. (This practice was quite common with Cedarwood; Flatt and Scruggs, among others, published Cedarwood songs under false names.) Jim Denny "almost demanded

that we cut some songs out of the Cedarwood catalog, but he didn't have nothing in there that we could sing. So we put that one in my wife's name, and 'I
Cried After You Left' as 'Faye Cunningham,' Ira's wife at the time." Helen Carter,
the composer of "The First One to Love You," was one of the daughters of
Mother Maybelle Carter, and was on the verge then of carving out her own
career as a soloist and a songwriter.

Sessions 14, 15, and 16   MAY 2, 3, AND 4, 1956

I'll Be All Smiles Tonight (A. P. Carter)	Cap EAP1 769 (EP)
In the Pines (Alan Riggs)	Cap EAP3 769 (EP)
What Is a Home without Love (Traditional)	Cap EAP2 769 (EP)
Mary of the Wild Moor (Traditional)	Cap T769 (LP)
The Knoxville Girl (Arr. Louvins)	Cap 4117
Kentucky (Carl Davis)	Cap EAP1 769 (EP)
Katie Dear (Bill and Earl Bolick)	Cap EAP1 769 (EP)
My Brother's Will (Ken Nelson)	Cap EAP1 769 (EP)
Take the News to Mother (Calloway-Callahan)	Cap EAP3 769 (EP)
Let Her Go, God Bless Her (Traditional)	Cap EAP2 769 (EP)
A Tiny Broken Heart	Cap EAP2 769 (EP)
Plenty of Everything but You (C & I Louvin)	Cap 3715
Cash on the Barrelhead (Ira and Charles Louvin)	Cap 3523

In spring 1956 Ken Nelson decided to try a Louvin Brothers LP, and to that
end they all began work on their first "concept" album, *Tragic Songs of Life.*
During May 1956 the brothers went into the Nashville studios to put down
some of their most powerful singing, as well as what were to be two of their
biggest singles.

"The Knoxville Girl" was part of the album but was not released as a single
until 1959. Then it spent seven weeks on the chart, going as high as number
seventeen. It too, though, became another Louvin classic that was far more
influential than its actual chart history indicates. The Louvins had been singing
it since they were young. "Maybe almost the first song we ever sang was 'The
Knoxville Girl,'" recalls Charlie. "It was the most requested song we ever sang,
audience-wise. That song even caused fights, you know. There's a cute story
about Ira. We were working Memphis, this was after we had come to the Opry

and were back in Memphis to do a date about 1957. The only place to change clothes was in the public restroom. We were in there trying to get our stage clothes on, shaving in the sink, and this drunk came in. He said, 'By God, I've drove four hundred miles to hear "The Knoxville Girl."' Of course, Ira was drinking about as much as he was, and he said, 'Well, I'll tell you what, friend; if you're that damn stupid you might as well get back in your car and go home 'cause you won't hear "The Knoxville Girl" tonight.' And he said, 'Well by God I better!' So later on from the audience he stood up and started hollering "The Knoxville Girl!" and Ira called him some bad names from the stage, and he refused to sing that song 'cause that man said 'You better.' If you'd leave Ira alone, naturally we would have done the song; but he was temperamental, like Ferlin Husky. If you tell Ferlin Husky you've traveled three hundred miles to see Simon Crum [his comedic alter ego] (and don't mention Ferlin), he'll just tell you, 'Well you won't see him tonight. 'Cause Simon don't do nothing that I don't tell him to do.' "

Why was there a two and a half year delay before Capitol issued the single? According to Charlie,

> We tried to, because of the audience reaction everywhere we'd gone, get Capitol to bring that out as a single. Almost from the time we cut it. And they said it was too morbid. It was too long. Too this and too that. And then they had great success with the Kingston Trio's "Tom Dooley," which was a five-minute song and just as tragic as "The Knoxville Girl." So they had a little change of heart: "maybe it's not too morbid, maybe it's not too long." So in the meantime, the Wilburn Brothers were getting as many requests for "The Knoxville Girl" where they went as we were. So they'd sing it. And they got to thinking, If this thing gets requested like this, I bet it'd sell. So lo and behold, they recorded it on Decca. They released it and they beat us out three days. When Capitol finally decided to release it as our single, they didn't know the Wilburns had cut it, the Wilburns didn't know we were going to release it as a single, so the records came out at the same time. Well, the Wilburns took arrangement copyright on the song, but we didn't when we cut it first in 1956, 'cause we didn't believe in stealing songs. But they took arrangement, and they collected the royalties off of Capitol for our record! But then later we went ahead and copyrighted the Louvin Brothers arrangement, so we would get paid at least for the singles, if not the album.
>
> That's an old English folk song; it's had several titles, "The Wentworth Girl," "The Oxford Girl," several more. Everybody in this country thinks we were talking

about Knoxville, Tennessee, because you've got the river there and everything that it says in the song. But we'd been singing the song all our life, almost every show we ever done.

"Mary of the Wild Moor" was another folk song they had known all their lives. "Like 'The Knoxville Girl,' it tends to build up," says Charlie. When he sings it today, Charlie often wonders about the subject—a young girl having a baby out of wedlock—and how different the reaction of society in that song is from society's reaction today, when the baby is often brought home and grandparents help raise it. "Our mother used to sing those old ballads," he remembers. "We had a lot of people that we were raised up with that were lovers of the folk music. The music changed from one holler to another, and so we'd visit these other people, and people would sing old songs that we hadn't heard. We would listen to them a couple of times, and being blessed with a pretty fair memory, we would take 'em back to our holler. And claim 'em for us. 'Katy Dear' was another in that *Tragic Songs* album, and it was a murder ballad, an 'I'll Die with the One I Like Best' type of song." The Louvins' mother would sing the old ballads unaccompanied, in the classic mountain style. "Her maiden name was Georgianne Wootten. She learned these songs from her mother, too; her father was a preacher, and I was named after him. You know, a preacher never follows another preacher, so I guess I was lucky there."

One of the songs that was not quite as traditional was "My Brother's Will." credited to Ken Nelson and Central Songs. "I don't know if he actually wrote it; he presented it to us. I like what the song says, and it fit the theme of the album."

Tragic Songs of Life was scheduled to be the brothers' first Capitol LP, and in fact their first LP, period. But Wesley Rose, says Charlie, "crafty old fox that he was," got wind of the impending Capitol release and rushed out a compilation of the old MGM sides on an LP and actually beat the Capitol set out. "The picture on the MGM album was even the picture that the drawing on 'Tragic Songs of Life' was made from."

Why did the brothers decide to make their first album a selection of old folk songs instead of some of the hotter new numbers like "I Don't Believe You've Met My Baby"? "Well, we came up with the title *Tragic Songs of Life*. Ira knew a lot more tragedy than I did . . . personal tragedy. He thrived when he lived in that music. I liked the songs too and the people where we worked and sang 'em at, we could just sit in the living room and sing those old tragic songs for five or six hours. Somebody might pee on themself for fear they might miss one if they went to the restroom. . . . As an artist, you will find yourself singing songs that are tried and tested and have worked before." When they brought the concept to Nelson, he didn't resist it; in fact, he said, "I'll have a song that'll fit that album."

Other songs fit the concept as well and incidentally paid tribute to some of the great brother duets of the past. "Kentucky" was popularized by both Karl and Harty and the Blue Sky Boys in the 1940s, while "Katie Dear" was an old traditional murder ballad that the Blue Sky Boys had harmonized and recorded. "I'll Be All Smiles Tonight" came from the Carter Family songbag, while "In the Pines," is one of the most venerable and complex folk lyrics in spite of its odd composer credits. (It is credited on this album to Alan Riggs but more frequently to Clayton McMichen.) "What Is a Home without Love?" was one of the Monroe Brothers' first Bluebird records back in 1936.

The Louvins finished out the session with two songs that were designed, not for the album, but as singles: "Plenty of Everything but You" and "Cash on the Barrelhead." Ira sang the latter as a solo, and Charlie did the solo on the former. "We had these two songs," recalls Charlie. "Couldn't get nobody else to record them, so we said, Next time we cut an album, we'll cut 'em. Ira wanted to cut 'Cash,' the other one was more my style. And people thought it was a signal, but it wasn't."

At that year's disc jockey convention, Eddie Hill, who was now doing some managing and booking for the brothers, helped come up with a device to plug the song. "We was in this room with the awards, and had a fifty-gallon barrel where the wooden lid comes up, and Ira had glued money—literally glued like silver dollars and half dollars. And they had free beer inside the barrel, but on top was 'Cash on the Barrelhead.'" The stunt must have helped—the song spent twelve weeks on the charts, going as high as number seven in the fall of 1956.

Session 17 JUNE 28, 1956

You're Running Wild (Ray Edenton-Don Winters)	Cap 3523
The New Partner Waltz (Ira and Charles Louvin)	Cap 3630

"You're Running Wild" became the flip side of "Cash on the Barrelhead" and like it spent twelve weeks on the charts, rising to No. 7, after it was released in September 1956. The song was written by Ray Edenton, the Louvins' favorite studio rhythm guitarist, and Don Winters. Winters was a tenor singer with Marty Robbins and lived in one of Robbins's houses, helping to take care of his horses and livestock. "I guess he and Ray wrote it together," says Charlie. "Ray pitched the song. It was a good number. Ray had a wife that claimed she was allergic to their child, so he had to raise it and feed it and change it. As a matter of fact, she also claimed she was allergic to him. But she wasn't allergic to a lot of people, and later he did get a divorce. That's the only divorce case I was ever a witness at. With my own eyes I seen the things she done. She toured, she was a singer, she toured with the Ernest Tubb group. . . . So when I found out she was trying to rip Ray, I went and gave a deposition. And when her lawyer read it and read it back to her and asked her if it was true, when she admitted it, he dropped the case. So Ray did completely raise the child, as a divorced parent." Charlie thinks this song was a direct result of his relationship with his wife. "It certainly fits." Ira drew cartoons advertising the new single.

Promotional cartoons by Ira

Sessions 18, 19   OCTOBER 28 AND OCTOBER 31, 1956

I Won't Have to Cross Jordan Alone (Traditional)	Cap EAP3 825 (EP)
Praying (Hazel Houser)	Cap 3770
Wait a Little Longer, Please Jesus (Hazel Houser-Chester Smith)	Cap EAP1 825 (EP)
This Little Light of Mine (Traditional)	Cap EAP3 825 (EP)
Steal Away and Pray (Charles and Ira Louvin)	Cap EAP3 825 (EP)
There's No Excuse (Charles and Ira Louvin)	Cap 3770
Are You Washed in the Blood (Traditional)	Cap EAP1 825 (EP)
Lord, I'm Coming Home (Traditional)	Cap EAP3 825 (EP)
Thankful (Ira and Charles Louvin)	Cap EAP1 825 (EP)

In November 1956, the Louvins were being managed by Xavier Cosse, the veteran Nashville booker and manager-husband of gospel great Martha Carson. They had won 1956 *Billboard* awards for Best Sacred Group, Best Singing Group, and Most Programmed Group. In the *Country Music Reporter* for November 10 of that year, Cosse announced that "all their sacred music henceforth will be sold only in album form." It was a concession to the recent secular hits such as "When I Stop Dreaming" and "Hoping That You're Hoping," but also a reflection of the changing role of the LP album in country music. On the heels of the *Tragic Songs of Life* LP, Nelson scheduled their first gospel concept album, *Nearer My God to Thee* (Capitol T825), which was released in early 1957.

The album saw the first time the Louvins recorded songs by a person who was to become one of their most effective writers, Hazel Houser. Houser provided for this session "Praying," as well as an older song she had written called "Wait a Little Longer, Please Jesus." (She would soon bring them "My Baby's Gone.") At this point, the Louvins had never met Hazel Houser. She was from Modesto, California, and published her songs through Central. "Ken would bring 'em. 'Here's a song you must record.' He didn't bring us any trash. He offered us a little deal, though; if you recorded any Central songs (later we put a hundred songs in Central, when we became nonexclusive with Acuff-Rose, the biggest mistake we ever made) he gave us an additional 20 percent of the publisher's part of the song. You get 50 percent of it, and then you'd get 20 percent of the publisher's, 10 percent of one hundred, which would make us get 60 percent of what the song made, instead of the fifty we got at Acuff-Rose. Of course, that was strictly Ken Nelson's word, and there was no paper on it at all. When Ira died, they just quit sending the extra 20 percent."

Charlie did not meet Hazel Houser until after Ira died and he found himself playing a date across the bay from Modesto. He described her as "a complex person," a little younger than Ira. He remembered her not as a full-time musician, but as "a working girl—she held down a job out there." She had written the standard "Wait a Little Longer, Please Jesus" in 1954 and had recorded it with singer Chester Smith for Capitol that year. "She was an avid Louvin Brothers fan," Charlie says, which partly explained why her songs were so very well suited to the Louvin style. "As a friend of Ken Nelson, she received everything that we recorded, probably before the radio stations got it."

Neither Charlie nor Ira were quick to claim old songs as their own; they had sung many of these gospel songs all their careers, and when they were not sure of the composers, they instructed Nelson to list them merely as "traditional." In the case of "I Won't Have to Cross Jordan Alone," the provenance was not all that old. The song was by Charles E. Durham and Thomas Ramsey and had first appeared in a 1934 Stamps-Baxter gospel songbook called *Leading Light*. In fact, it had been dedicated to V. O. Stamps by its composer, Durham, and had become popular with the gospel quartets that once ranged the South. "Lord, I'm Coming Home" was an old chesnut by William J. Kirkpatrick, a former Civil War fife major who also wrote the familiar "Jesus Saves." "Lord, I'm Coming Home" first appeared in a Philadelphia songbook called *Winning Songs* in 1892. "Are You Washed in the Blood" was from the pen of Elisha Albright Hoffman, an evangelical minister from the Midwest who published it first in a gospel/Sunday school songbook in 1878.

Sessions 20 and 21 MAY 1 AND 2, 1957

Take Me Back into Your Heart (Gene Autry-Fred Rose)	Cap T 910 (LP)
Here Today and Gone Tomorrow (Wally Fowler)	Cap T 910 (LP)
We Could (Felice Bryant)	Cap T 910 (LP)
Tennessee Waltz (Redd Stewart-Pee Wee King)	Cap T 910 (LP)
Too Late (Jimmy Wakeley)	Cap T 910 (LP)
Are You Teasing Me (Ira and Charles Louvin)	Cap T 910 (LP)
Nobody's Darling but Mine (Jimmie Davis)	Cap T 910 (LP)
Don't Let Your Sweet Love Die (Clarke Van Ness-Zeke Manners)	Cap T 910 (LP)
I Wonder Where You Are Tonight (Johnny Bond)	Cap T 910 (LP)

Why Not Confess (Ralph Hamrick)	Cap T 910 (LP)
Making Believe (Jimmy Work)	Cap T 910 (LP)
Have I Stayed Away Too Long (Frank Loesser)	Cap T 910 (LP)

The next album, *Ira and Charlie*, issued in 1958, was recorded in two marathon sessions in May 1957. It, too, was novel in that it featured a series of country standards by other modern country writers: Felice Bryant, Jimmy Wakeley, Johnny Bond, and Jimmy Work. At first glance, it might appear that the inclusion of this material was an attempt by Nelson and Capitol to show off the brothers' versatility and to push them even more into the mainstream of Grand Ole Opry-style country music. Yet, Charlie recalls, it was the brothers themselves who continued to be free to select not only the songs but the themes of their albums.

Some of the songs here had a bluegrass inflection. "Don't Let Your Sweet Love Die" became a hit in 1961 for Reno and Smiley, and "I Wonder Where You Are Tonight" was to be recorded by Bill Monroe in 1966. Bobby Bare took "Have I Stayed Away Too Long" (by Broadway composer Frank Loesser) to the charts in 1964. "Why Not Confess" was the last real hit by The Blue Sky Boys, while "Making Believe" was a hit for Work and for Kitty Wells. Of older vintage were the Gene Autry favorite "Take Me Back into Your Heart," Jimmie Davis's 1934 version of the old nineteenth-century lament "Nobody's Darling but Mine," and the 1950s favorite "Tennessee Waltz," which sounds surprisingly good in Louvin harmony.

Session 22   MAY 7, 1957

Call Me (Ira and Charles Louvin)	Cap 3804
I Wish You Knew (Ira and Charles Louvin)	Cap 3804
Dog Sled (Ira and Charles Louvin)	Cap 3871
When I Loved You (Ira and Charles Louvin)	Cap 3871

"Dog Sled" was another song for which Ira liked to draw cartoons for use in mailers and promotions. "Ira wanted to cut that as a solo, so he worked up all them whip crackings and whistles and the dogs. Hank Thompson had just had a pretty good record on 'Squaws Along the Yukon,' so Ira came up with this little song. The closest thing he's ever been to a dog sled was in a world atlas map." "Call Me" was a real sleeper from this session—a slow waltz in the classic Louvin style that was amazing in the fact that it even appeared in the midst of the rock and roll revolution that was challenging Nashville's traditional sounds. Not surprisingly, the single that was released did little.

"When I Loved You" and "I Wish You Knew" rounded out the session. It was the last time Paul Yandell added his distinctive guitar work to a Louvin recording—he soon left to serve in the armed forces. This was also the last session before Ken Nelson would decide he didn't like Ira's mandolin solos, a critique that put a damper on Ira's solo breaks for some time to come. "I Wish You Knew" featured Ira singing lead on the verse, then switching to tenor for the chorus.

The chart hits now started coming regularly: "I Don't Believe You've Met My Baby" (January 1956), "Hoping That You're Hoping" (May 1956), and "You're Running Wild" and "Cash on the Barrelhead" (September 1956). By the end of the year, Xavier Cosse had announced that hencefore the brothers would issue gospel songs only in album form. They went out on package tours with other Opry stars—a far cry from the rural church and schoolhouse circuit they had done in Memphis. They appeared with Hank Snow, Justin Tubb, Ernest Tubb, the Carter Sisters, and did over one hundred days' work with Elvis Presley. "We worked dates with him from the Carolinas to Virginia, to Florida, even over to Texas," Charlie recalls. Elvis's mother was a fan of the Louvins from their Memphis days, and Charlie and Betty still stopped by to give her new releases. (Elvis himself once told a reporter in later years that the Louvins were his favorite duet act.) During weekends in the fall of 1956, Presley left the tour to go to New York and Hollywood for appearances on "The Ed Sullivan Show." A dispute with Colonel Tom Parker over payment for extra shows he added to the tour, and an ugly scene in which Ira told off Presley caused an end to the tour. (Backstage in North Carolina, Elvis began playing the piano and singing a gospel song. "This is really my favorite kind of music," he commented. Ira was standing nearby and took offense. "If that's your favorite music, why don't you do that out yonder?" he shouted, "instead of that trash?" Presley lamely responded, "When I'm out there, I do what they want to hear; when I'm back here, I do what I want to do." Charlie recalls that things almost came to blows before both men quieted down. One effect, he thinks was that if Elvis had ever had any ideas about recording a Louvin Brothers gospel song, he dropped them.)

By the middle of 1957, the brothers had themselves a new manager, Preston Temple, and Ira had a new wife, his third, Faye Cunningham. Faye was Kitty Wilson's sister. In May, Temple negotiated a deal for the brothers with the

Ira and Charlie with their early inspiration, Roy Acuff

Wheeling (West Virginia) "Jamboree," and they planned another move. Their formal resignation from the Opry took place on May 28, and the Opry brass—Dee Kilpatrick, Roy Acuff, and others—even threw them a going-away party. "People have reported a story that we left the Opry in a huff, because of the supposed competition from the Everly Brothers. Nothing could be further from the truth. There wasn't a jealous bone in nobody's body toward the Everly Brothers." The truth was that the manager of the Wheeling show had offered them a decent wage if they would transfer there and make the show twenty times a year. Like all other singers, the Louvins were just getting scale for the weekly Opry shows, and this deal sounded better. When they got to Wheeling, though, they had trouble even finding a place to live; then they learned that there had been a mix-up, that the Jamboree was only paying twelve dollars a show scale itself. "We told him," says Charlie, "that that was not the kind of deal we talked about—that there was no way we were going to work for that kind of money.

So we went back to Nashville." They were a little concerned about getting back on the Opry, but Temple was a close friend to Dee Kilpatrick, who had just taken over at the Opry. "He went to Dee and said, 'I've made a terrible mistake with this deal. Can you let them back on the Opry?' And he did. We couldn't have been gone to West Virginia more than a few weeks."

Ira, meanwhile, was getting caught up in more and more personal problems. He was becoming known as a ladies' man, and between (and during) marriages had a number of relationships with people around the Opry. For a time he was seeing Maxine Brown, and for her birthday gave her a song, possibly "Looking Back to See." (Maxine Brown, for the record, denies that Ira wrote the song and recalls that it was she who came up with the idea. She agrees that Ira provided her and The Browns other songs, including "I Thought You Thought," which The Browns recorded for Fabor-Abbott in 1955—a song that did bear Ira's name on the credits.) Later Ira began seeing Ernest Tubb's daughter Elaine ("Scooter"), and this caused friction between the brothers and Tubb, who didn't approve. After Bobbie got her divorce from Ira, she routinely had him arrested for overdue child support and alimony; the brothers kept a little lockbox in their house where they put spare cash, and whenever Ira got arrested and had no money to pay his way out, Preston Temple would go to his house, dig into the box, and eventually come up with enough change to pay the sheriff. "Sometimes it would take an hour and a half, two hours, to count out the change," recalls Charlie. "A lot of it would be in quarters."

MY BABY'S GONE

In the late 1950s, Ira's volatile temper got worse. When he was not drinking he was fine, but when he was drinking, one band member said, "it was sorta like walking on eggs." One minute Ira was the fun-loving, good-time practical joker; the next, some casual remark set him off and he flew into a rage. Another sideman described Ira as having a split personality like Dr. Jekyll and Mr. Hyde, a split that went far beyond the surface split between gospel singer and hard-drinking womanizer. "It seemed that Ira was jealous of anyone that was real normal," said another band member. In 1955, the brothers were invited to take part in the filming of the color films that were being done in Nashville by Ganaway productions—the only really good film performances of many 1950s country artists. The Louvins appeared in a couple of the shows, but Ira got upset about something somebody said, and they appeared in no more. As a result, there are few surviving films of the Louvins at their peak.

Ira became known for throwing tantrums onstage during shows. "He didn't like to use the best mandolins sometimes," recalls Charlie. "And a lot of times his mandolin would go out of tune during a show. He'd just turn around from the mike and throw it as hard as he could to the back of the stage. Then he'd just walk off stage, and the band and I would have to finish the best we could—instrumentals and solos from me. There ain't no telling how many times he pulled that—I can think of at least a dozen times. Sometimes he'd smash the mandolin, and then later try to repair it. You'd have to make an excuse to the booker, tell him Ira must have gotten sick and didn't feel like working—the only thing you had to go with. It seems like it always happened when it never should have happened, where there might be 95 percent family people in the audience. 'Cause family-oriented people are not satisfied by you saying, 'That was the booze talking, that wasn't really him.' They'll just take that it was rude and nasty and not come back. If that happened in a club, where there was a lot of drinking going on, they'd just have come up and helped him stomp it."

One incident that almost everybody remembers occurred on a trip to Oklahoma in late 1959. Jimmy Dickens and Jimmy C. Newman were on the show with the Louvins, and the brothers went on in the middle of the show. After a couple of numbers, Ira stopped, held up his mandolin, thumped it, and sailed it off toward the dressing room door. It bounced and landed back on the side of the stage, in full view of the audience. Furious, Ira stomped it a few times on stage but somehow couldn't really splinter it. So he carted it back to the dressing room and continued to attack it. Dickens was in the room and watched with bemused detachment. Finally he grabbed the instrument, wedged it up against an iron radiator, and told Ira, "Stomp right here, and I believe you can break that neck." (In all his stomping, Ira had never really destroyed the neck of an instrument.) This gesture made Ira even angrier, and he told Dickens to butt out. "If I want to stomp my mandolin, it's my mandolin, and I don't need any help!"

Ira had already had to have Faye, his wife, air ship him one mandolin on the tour because he had destroyed one earlier. Now, with his second mandolin in tatters, he announced that he was quitting the tour and going home. He put his mandolin pieces in a paper bag and stalked out; Dickens offered to send a young man named Roger Miller to Nashville for a replacement, but Charlie told him to hold off. Then, while they were loading their gear into the Louvins' Oldsmobile outside, Ira stepped on the suit of a band member, Jimmy Capps, and Charlie lost his temper. Ira was never a fighter and was taken aback when Charlie tore into him and started beating his head against the curb. The others pulled them apart, and things seemed quiet again. Then, on the way out of town, Ira reached down and pulled out a little .22 pistol. Nobody knew whether he was bluffing, whether he intended to use it on Dickens (who was sitting beside him), or whether he was going to use it on himself. Nobody even knew that Ira had a gun, and everybody froze. Dickens reached over and grabbed the gun. "Man, you don't need the gun," he said. "Give me that." He emptied the shells out of it, and one of the other men in the car threw them out the window.

Things calmed down later that night, and Ira called again to have another mandolin flown in. (He later managed to repair the one in the sack.) "It would have been nice if Ira had carried two or three mandolins," said Charlie. "On a month's tour; it might take that many to get through the tour."

Session 23   AUGUST 1, 1958

My Baby's Gone (Hazel Houser)   Cap 4055

She Didn't Even Know I Was Gone (Ira and Charles Louvin)   Cap 3974

My Baby Came Back (Ira and Charles Louvin)   Cap 3974

Are You Wasting My Time (Ira and Charles Louvin)   Cap EAP 1 1106

Little of all this turmoil, however, was evident in the next Capitol session, held late that summer. It yielded two masterpieces, "My Baby's Gone" and "My Baby Came Back." Curiously, it has always been assumed that "My Baby Came Back" was a sequel to "My Baby's Gone," and Ira quite probably wrote it as such, but in fact "My Baby Came Back" was released on a single *before* "My Baby's Gone." But the session was also the scene of a traumatic confrontation that was to change the sound of the Louvins' music.

"My Baby's Gone" became the best-known song from the session and the title song from the 1960 album that included most of the songs recorded here and in the following two sessions. The song stayed on the charts for a long time—some twenty-two weeks—during which it hovered between no. 18 and no. 22, eventually peaking at no. 9. "That song sold 258,000 copies," recalls Charlie. "We had proof that it sold 258,000 because we owned the [song rights to] B side of the single, 'Lorene.' At that time Wilma Lee and Stoney Cooper had recorded a Louvin Brothers song called 'More Love.' We got paid, and if there was anybody that was honest, it was Acuff-Rose. We got paid for 5,000 records on 'More Love,' and it went to no. 1 and stayed there three weeks. We sold 258,000 of 'My Baby's Gone,' and it never went to that position."

"My Baby's Gone" was not a Louvin composition but came from the pen of California writer Hazel Houser. Ken Nelson had brought the song to the brothers. Houser specialized in writing gospel songs, several of which the brothers had recorded (see session listings above), but Nelson had been encouraging her to try writing some non-gospel material. She did, but "My Baby's Gone" was Houser's only "secular" effort the brothers recorded.

With the new rock and roll revolution making devastating inroads into the country scene (both in terms of record sales and bookings), Ira felt increasing pressure to try his hand at rock and roll material. He was versatile enough to bring it off, and did so with "She Didn't Even Know I Was Gone," a back-beat teen romance ballad that was good enough for Capitol to try as a single.

More important, though, was an event that occurred in the studio during the cutting of this session. Charlie remembers it vividly. "Of all the great things Ken Nelson did for the Louvin Brothers, he almost destroyed them. It was after Presley had hit, and Carl Perkins, and a few others, and they were changing the face of country music completely, and we were in the studio fixing to cut 'My Baby's Gone.' He said, 'I believe that the mandolin is hurting the sales of Louvin Brothers records.' Well, this was an instrument that Ira had spent the better part of twenty years on, and I thought he had become very proficient on it. And here is what he thought his best friend in the world, who wouldn't give him no bad advice, was telling him: basically [that] he was the reason that the songs were slowing down. Which wasn't true. It wasn't just Louvin Brothers material that was hurting—Webb Pierce, for instance, was swept completely out of the business, and a lot of people that had had a dozen number ones in a row. Just blown away. So at that point, Ira laid the mandolin down, never to take another break on a record. He refused to take a break. Let the piano do it, or let the steel do it, or let the lead do it, I don't want to stop any more records from selling; he kind of rubbed it in the rest of the time and became an extreme heavy drinker. And in a period of six years went through three more marriages. So I credit Ken Nelson with making Louvin Brothers and also destroying Louvin Brothers. It's hard to swallow. It's like the story they tell about a guy who was commissioned to paint a picture of Jesus. He looked everywhere for a subject. He finally found a subject and painted it, to show the tenderness and all this, in Jesus' face, and some years later he was asked to do another picture. And he looked all over the world for a face to do this and finally found the man in prison. And he painted this picture, and finally the guy was kind of irritated. He said, 'You act like you don't know me.' And he said, 'I don't know you.' And he said, 'You painted me ten years ago.' So that would show you what going from good to the other end of the scale would make a man look like. The same [face] was used to paint Christ, and then a very sinister person."

Session 24   AUGUST 4, 1958

My Curly Headed Baby (Traditional)	Cap 4255
Lorene (Ira and Charles Louvin)	Cap 4055
I Wish It Had Been a Dream (Ira and Charles Louvin)	Cap 4117
While You're Cheating on Me (Ira and Charles Louvin)	Cap 4200

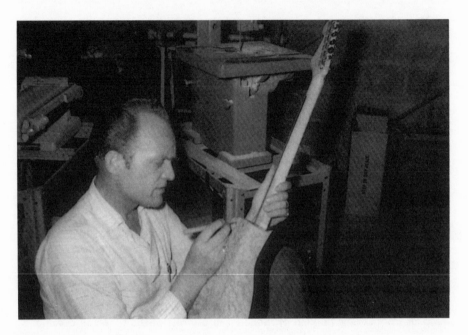

Ira in his guitar workshop

"My Curly Headed Baby" was the Louvin version of a duet classic recorded and popularized by the Callahan Brothers, radio stars from the 1930s and 1940s. The Callahans hailed from North Carolina and made up the song from a series of old fragments; they recorded it in 1934, and it has remained identified with them ever since.

"Lorene" was named after one of the Louvin sisters (one who in fact eventually recorded with them: see session 48). "That song came from a silly thing: she was married to this old boy and they separated and the boy would make silly remarks around to Ira. So he just picked up those silly remarks, you know, 'Lorene, write me a letter,' and turned it into a song."

"While You're Cheating on Me" supposedly was about Ira's third wife, Faye Cunningham. "That's a good song," says Charlie. "I'm surprised that some of the artists of today haven't picked that song up."

"I Wish It Had Been a Dream": "We tried to do a different thing on that, using the same kind of off-beat we used on 'Every Time You Leave.' It was different from anything that we had done." Although it was issued as a single, the song attracted little attention.

Session 25   AUGUST 5, 1958

If I Could Only Win Your Love (Ira and Charles Louvin)   Cap T 1106 (LP)

You're Learning (Ira and Charles Louvin)   Cap 4255

"If I Could Only Win Your Love": "If you heard the Louvin Brothers record of it and then heard what Emmylou did to it, you'd have trouble believing that that was the same song. To me, it just clobbers my mind to know the way some of the young people hear the old songs. I think it's great. I don't really have a story on the song, but Ira was, at least in his own mind, a ladies' man, and I think this was wrote about somebody he didn't score with. That was actually a new song when we recorded it." It was in fact recorded in August 1958, not issued as a single, and not copyrighted by Acuff-Rose until 1959. "Acuff-Rose would not copyright a song until they got notification of a record release date. They didn't even have the lead sheets made until the record company says, 'Send us a mechanical license on such-and-such a song.'" Surprisingly, "Win Your Love" was never issued as a single and saw the light of day only on the 1959 album *Country Love Ballads*.

Of "You're Learning" Charlie says only, "Good song, poor arrangement." It was eventually issued on the flip side of "Curly Headed Baby," and was one of the Louvin songs Capitol chose for its 1990 reissue, *Hillbilly Music Thank God*.

Sessions 26 and 27   AUGUST 6 AND 7, 1958

Blue From Now On (Jim Leisy)   Cap 4200

Today (Hank Thompson)   Cap T 1106 (LP)

My Heart Was Trampled on the Street (Ira and Charles Louvin)   Cap T 1106 (LP)

Send Me the Pillow You Dream On (Hank Locklin)   Cap T 1106 (LP)

On My Way to the Show (Ira and Charles Louvin)   Cap T 1106 (LP)

Read What's in My Heart (Dell Shirley)   Cap T 1106 (LP)

Red Hen Hop (Ira and Charles Louvin)   Cap T 1106 (LP)

She Will Get Lonesome (Ira and Charles Louvin)   Cap T 1106 (LP)

I Wonder If You Know (Ella Barrett)   Cap T 1106 (LP)

Blue (Freddie Hart)   Cap T 1106 (LP)

By now the Louvins were in full stride with their career: touring, radio, and regular sessions for one of the country's biggest record companies. By modern standards, the speed with which they ground out albums is amazing. Charlie recollects: "You would have three hours to cut fifteen minutes of recorded music—which can be as much as five songs. Ira and I used to cut an album in two sessions. Then it became complicated: adding voices and more and more music. First thing you know, you had seventeen people in the studio, each eligible to make a mistake. Before it was just me and Ira. And we rehearsed it so much we didn't make a whole lot of them [mistakes]. Even though, Ken had to step in several times. Ira was a perfectionist and he might do as many as thirty-two takes. We'd just sing ourselves to death on the first song. Finally Ken would say, 'Wait a minute, I just loved the way take 3 sounded.' And Ira would say, 'Well, I missed so-and-so there,' and he'd say, 'Hell, it didn't bother me. That's the one I'm gonna release.'"

In early August 1958 Nelson lined the brothers up to do not one but *two* albums in one huge marathon session. First they would do a series of country favorites that would be called *Country Love Ballads*; next they would go right on

Publicity photo, ca. 1956

to their next gospel set, which would be called *Satan Is Real*. Nelson hoped to have no fewer than twenty-four songs for the albums, plus four additional cuts for singles, recorded in the span of seven days.

Even though the liner notes to *Country Love Ballads* implied that all the songs from this session were favorites that the Louvins had been singing on personal appearances, only one of them had really been a bonafide hit. That was Hank Locklin's "Send Me the Pillow You Dream On," which had made the charts only three months earlier. "Blue" was an early Freddie Hart song, sent to the duo through Central Songs. Charlie says, "I've been a Freddie Hart fan since I first met him, and I heard his record of this, and felt it would make a good harmony song. We saved it, and then one day when the time was right and the album was right, we threw it in there."

Sessions 28, 29, and 30   AUGUST 8, 9, AND 10, 1958

The Angels Rejoiced Last Night (Ira and Charles Louvin)	Cap T 1277 (LP)
Dying from Home and Lost (S. M. Brown)	Cap T 1277 (LP)
Satan's Jeweled Crown (Edgar L. Edens)	Cap T 1277 (LP)
The River of Jordan (Hazel Houser)	Cap 4112, T 1277 (LP)
I'm Ready to Go Home (Hazel Houser)	Cap T 1277 (LP)
The Kneeling Drunkard's Plea (Helen, Anita, June, and	
Maybelle Carter)	Cap T 1277 (LP)
Satan Is Real (Ira and Charles Louvin)	Cap T 1277 (LP)
The Christian Life (Ira and Charles Louvin)	Cap T 1277 (LP)
Are You Afraid to Die (Ira and Charles Louvin)	Cap T 1277 (LP)
He Can Be Found (Ella Barrett-Faye Cunningham)	Cap 4112, T 1277 (LP)
There's a Higher Power (Ira and Charles Louvin)	Cap T 1277 (LP)
The Drunkard's Doom (Ira and Charles Louvin)	Cap T 1277 (LP)

The next three days were spent on what would be the brothers' best-known and most colorful gospel album, *Satan Is Real*. Much of the initial interest in the album stemmed from the bizarre and distinctive cover, which showed the brothers in white linen suits crouched before a huge image of Satan, surrounded by the fires of hell. This was, of course, by design. For some time the brothers had taken an active interest in designing their own LP covers; they had, for instance, submitted a photo mock-up and design that was used for the *My Baby's Gone* album cover. About the *Satan Is Real* cover Charlie recalls: "Ira built that

[set]. The devil was twelve feet tall, built out of plywood. We went to this rock quarry and then took old tires and soaked them in kerosene, got them to burn good. It had just started to sprinkle rain when we got that picture taken. Those rocks, when they get hot, they blow up. They were throwing pieces of rock up into the air." Things almost got out of hand during the photography, and the brothers barely escaped injury. The result, though, was one of the most startling album covers in country music history.

The title cut, "Satan Is Real," spotlights a recitation by Ira to the effect that "it's sweet to know that God is real . . . but Satan is real, too." The idea came from a country church the brothers had attended in Alabama when an old man stood up in the middle of a revival service and made the same point. The close, tender harmony that links the Louvins to the Delmores is heard on "The Christian Life" and "Dying from Home and Lost." The former was a piece soon picked up by gospel and country groups and eventually recorded by the folk-rock group The Byrds, giving it even more exposure. The latter is an old, old gospel piece that was popularized by the Blue Sky Boys. "Satan's Jeweled Crown" is another from the set that was revived later—this time by West Coast singer Nicollette Larsen, who had a hit with it in the 1980s. The more strident, soaring, urgent harmony that was the brothers' trademark appears in "The River of Jordan," "Are You Afraid to Die," and Hazel Houser's master-piece, "I'm Ready to Go Home." Throughout, Jimmy Capps's Merle Travis-styled guitar frames the vocals, and Ira's mandolin is happily in evidence throughout. "The Kneeling Drunkard's Plea" is noteworthy in that it sports a vocal trio; the brothers were joined by general session handyman and Grandpa Jones band member George McCormick, who never quite forgot the experience. "You haven't lived until you've had to sing the third part of 'The Kneeling Drunkard's Plea' with Ira and Charlie Louvin," he laughs.

Session 31   NOVEMBER 5, 1959

I See a Bridge (Ira and Charles Louvin)	Cap 4359
Just Suppose (Ira and Charles Louvin)	Cap 4359
The Stagger (Ira and Charles Louvin)	Cap 4331
Nellie Moved to Town (Ira and Charles Louvin)	Cap 4331

By this session, the brothers were placing almost all their songs with Central Songs; they had become nonexclusive with Acuff-Rose, and at Nelson's request were placing many of their newer pieces with "his" company.

One of the more uncharacteristic of all Louvin songs was "The Stagger." By late 1959, new teenage dance fads like the Madison and the Hully Gully were sweeping through the dance parties—and record charts—and in 1961 Chubby Checker introduced the ultimate dance fad, the Twist. "It was when the music had just gone haywire," says Charlie. Ira wrote out the steps to this new dance he invented, the Stagger. "It wasn't really a new dance," says Charlie. "I just did a two step to it. But Ira could do it pretty well."

"'I See a Bridge' was written because of something my sister Lorene said. We were coming toward Stevenson, Alabama, and when you come right to the top of the mountain, you can see that new bridge down there. Well, that used to be a ferry when we were kids, and if you went across the river there you had to ride a ferry. My sister Lorene would drink, and she was a happy drinker, and she'd had a few, and so when we came around that curve, she hollered, 'Oh look, I see a bridge,' a way to go over it. And, hell, he just like that, he stopped the car right there and just wrote it."

Most of the time Ira wrote from something like that, something that really happened. "If you could give him a title, he'd write it as quick as you could write your wife a note that you were going to the store to get some milk."

On the flip side of "The Stagger" was a lovely slow song called "Nellie Moved to Town." "That was my first love," Charlie muses. "Her name was Nell Cook. I seriously thought I was in love. It didn't work out that way. I went to the army in the early part of 1946; she wanted to get married right then. Well, I had this little bet with my daddy, we talked about some of the other kids, two sisters that got married when they were thirteen, one got married when she was fourteen, another one fifteen, to get away from home. [My dad] was pretty strict. Ira married when he was seventeen, was a father before he was eighteen. My father said, 'Kids today, too young to marry. You've got sense enough not to marry until you are twenty-two or better.' I said, 'How old were you?' and he said, 'I was twenty-two.' And I said, 'Well, I'll be older than you were before I get married.' I did get married the year I was twenty-two. But, getting back, she wanted to get married and I knew too many war wives that anybody could have fun with, and I didn't want to leave one of them home. What she did as a single girl would be her business.

"She corresponded with me the whole time I was in. Sweetest letters you ever seen. When I came back, before I even went home to see my Mom and Dad, I went to Chattanooga, to that address where she'd been writing from. It was a shotgun type house with a thing right down the middle, which meant that one family lived on one side, one on the other. So here was a baby's play pen on the front porch and a baby's in there, damn near a year old. I didn't know whose baby it was, so I stepped up to the door and knocked on the door with my cigarette lighter, a big Zippo, and here she came to the door. Just before taking hold of her, just about to hug her neck completely off, and I heard jolly green giant steps. Somebody you could tell was big. This guy walks up, about this much taller than she was, and she said, 'Oh, I want you to meet my husband.' I could have fell through a crack in the floor. She'd been married for over a year. All the time she wrote those letters, she was married. But I'm kind of glad. She's gone through eight husbands by now." The song itself had been written by 1950, "but until the Everly Brothers came along and gave us an excuse to smooth the music, so to speak, we had no use for 'Nelly'; it wasn't our style. But in 1958, with the Everlys hitting so good, there was a possibility that we could have turned something around with that. But it didn't happen."

Session 32   MARCH 23, 1960

| **What a Change One Day Can Make** (Grady Cole) | Cap 4430 |
| **Ruby's Song** (Ira and Charles Louvin) | Cap 4395 |

"What a Change One Day Can Make" came from the pen of Georgian Grady Cole, composer of the classic "Tramp on the Street." In fact, next to that familiar song, "What a Change" was about Cole's most popular song. The Louvins never knew Grady personally, though they heard him on the radio, especially when he was broadcasting from Rome, Georgia. "We heard Grady and admired his work," says Charlie, "and that song was a part of our family for about as long as I can remember. I guess the way things were changing right about then [in the late 1950s] reminded us to record that song."

"Ruby's Song" is one that Charlie classifies with "Red Hen Hop" and "The Stagger" as one of the "sillier" songs they did. "Ruby is the ugliest girl that ever lived, about. She lived about two miles from where we were raised. Her brother played pretty good fiddle and would go a lot of places with Ira and I. He's the guy that could go in the house and say, 'I need to shave before we can go over there and play.' Go in the house, and of course we didn't have electric lights and he didn't want to light the lamp. So he'd get a little water and whip up his shavin' mug and put that all over his face and take his straight razor and hit it a couple of times, and he did a dang good shave. He'd feel everything. But he had the ugliest sister, and just for a joke Ira wrote this [within] hearing distance of the cotton gin and a thirty-minute walk to Ruby's; it was accurate." As it turned out, Ruby took it in good humor; she came to a recent Louvin festival at Henagar, Alabama, came up on the stage, and told Charlie, "You know me. You wrote a song about me! I'm Ruby!"

SCARED OF THE BLUES

Ira's violent streak took an even uglier turn a couple of years later, in 1961, in Nashville. This time Ira and Faye, his third wife, got into a serious argument. Charlie recalls: "It seems like Ira and Faye always moved into the same neighborhood we bought a house in, and they would always call on us when they got to drinking and got to fighting. One night around midnight I'd get a call from Ira saying, 'I've locked myself in the bathroom and she's got a knife and is trying to kill me,' and the next night about midnight we'd get a call from Faye saying, 'I've locked myself in the bedroom and he's at the door trying to kill me.' So I vowed I was going to move far enough away that if they called me it would take so long to get there that one of them really would be dead by the time I got there, and did: found a house out near Fairview (near Nashville). Then one night I got a call from Shot Jackson; 'It's finally happened, Charlie,' he said. 'Faye shot Ira and he's in the hospital and they say he may die.' Shot was always pulling practical jokes like this, and I thought this was another one, and said, 'Okay, Shot, thanks a lot. Give me a call if he dies.' Then thirty minutes later I got a call from the Madison Hospital; they needed to admit Ira, and had to have one sign for him to be good for the payment. I went up there, but by the time I got there Smiley Wilson had already gotten there and signed him in. We learned that Ira was trying to choke Faye with a telephone cord, and she got loose and ran for her bed. She kept a little .22 caliber pistol there, had it loaded with .22 shorts, and she fired it at Ira—in fact, she emptied it into him, all five shots."

They worked on him in the hospital that night and got two of the bullets out, but three were too close to the spine. They couldn't get them out, and they put some kind of a seal around them. In fact, Ira carried those slugs in his back until the day he died. The police went to see Faye, and she told them, "If the son of a bitch don't die, I'll shoot him again!" The story—and the quote—got

Ira and Faye (L), Charlie and
Betty (R)

in the newspaper and made the nationwide broadcast of Paul Harvey, the radio
commentator. Harvey ended his story with the quote and then added, "And
he's still alive." From his hospital bed, Ira told Charlie, "The bitch is crazy. She's
got to be put away." Agreeing that Faye might well try again, Charlie managed
to get a court order committing her to a mental institution (she had been in
the hospital with head injuries from the fight). In the meantime, the Opry was
getting nervous about all the bad publicity and asked Charlie and Ira to stay off
the air for three or four weeks until it all blew over.

It didn't blow over easily. Smiley and Kitty (Faye's sister) went to Roy Acuff
and asked him to help persuade Charlie to rescind his action and get Faye out.
"It turned out it was a lot harder to get her out of the mental hospital than it
was to get her in," said Charlie. (He resented being blamed for the situation
since he had only been following Ira's suggestion.) Finally Acuff himself, who
knew the governor fairly well, had to make a personal appeal to him to get him
to sign a release order for Faye. "She waited until Ira was back on his feet, and
then she left," says Charlie.

Personal problems were not the only sources of tension for the brothers by the late 1950s. Like most mainstream country acts, the Louvins found that rock and roll was causing their bookings and their record sales to drop off. Ira was versatile enough to respond to the rock and roll challenge and tried teen-flavored pieces like "Dog Sled" (1957) and "The Stagger" (1959). These songs were not really successful and irritated many of the act's traditional fans; even today, a recent article referred to such sides as the "low point" in the Louvins' career. More important was an incident in April 1958, when Ken Nelson was trying to find a way to jump-start Louvin record sales. His statement that he thought Louvin records were not selling well because of the high profile of the mandolin on them hurt Ira deeply. He had worked hard at his mandolin playing and was proud of the fact that he was one of the better players in Nashville. After this incident, Ira refused to play mandolin on many records, confining it to specific gospel tracks.

The brothers also began to do occasional recording sessions with other groups. Ira, for instance, sang on the harmony for Ray Price's 1956 hit "Wasted Words" (Columbia); Ray and Ira were old fishing buddies, and Ira came along to the session of June 22, 1956, and may have sung on an unissued track from the date, the Louvin song "Are You Wasting My Time?" In 1959 Ira sang with the Osborne Brothers on their version of the brothers' song "A Message to Your Heart" for MGM. Ira also added his mandolin to a special SESAC album of Nashville instrumentalists and reportedly helped out on several of the early recordings by the Browns. Fans of his distinctive mandolin style have suggested he is heard on a number of other sides by people with whom he worked, but further research is needed to confirm this assertion. One persistent story around Nashville even has Ira playing and singing a famous vintage television commercial for Tennessee Pride country sausage.

By 1959, most of the Louvins' backup band members had left as well. Paul Yandell was about to be drafted in the fall of 1958, and it was important to find a replacement who could play in his style. The Louvins eventually came upon Jimmy Capps, a guitarist from North Carolina. He was working out of Wilson with two men who specialized in Louvin songs, Tommy Hagen and Buck Jones. Capps had been "in love" with the Louvin Brothers' gospel music since he was a teenager and had developed a guitar style quite similar to Yandell's; it wasn't a real thumb style, but it was a good single-string style that sounded similar. Yandell heard Capps, auditioned him, and recommended that the Louvins hire him. Capps and new bass player Junior Huskey did their first recording session

in March 1960. (Tommy Hagen later joined Charlie as a harmony singer after
the breakup of the brothers in 1963.) Capps stayed with the Louvins until 1962,
when he was drafted as well.

Those who knew Ira well realized that his temper explosions, his violence,
his drinking, his quicksilver personality, and his womanizing were only the sensational part of the story. Ira continued to write some of the best songs in
the music and was generous about touching up and rewriting songs sent in by
others, such as "Satan's Jeweled Crown." He wrote songs with incredible ease,
and for a time had a little reel-to-reel tape recorder he could plug into the
cigarette lighter in their car. Often as Charlie drove on long trips, Ira would sit
in the back and compose songs, singing them onto the tape.

Although they had their bad moments—they were coming more and more
often by the early 1960s—Charlie and Ira amazed people with their musical
rapport, by their ability to merely glance at each other and pass signals about
a new key change or a turnaround in a piece. In some cases, Ira would get the
idea for a song and then he and Charlie would work it out together; at other

Promotional
shot

times, he would bring the rough draft of the song to Charlie. "He'd say, 'Get out your guitar and see what you think of this.' We'd lay the handwritten words down, he would say what key it was in, and he'd kick it off. You had to antici-pate, but when you get so close together, you know pretty well what a person's gonna do. By the kickoff, I'd know where my lead was. He wasn't unpredictable to me. I could look at him and tell if he was fixing to take the lead on a song and I was gonna take the low tenor on it. . . . Sometimes it wouldn't work out the first time, and most times, unless he was really hooked on the song, it just got thrown away. 'Probably wasn't worth a damn anyway,' he'd say. Sometimes somebody'd go back around and get the paper and straighten it out and we'd work it out later, and have a good song."

Charlie, for his part, had emerged as the businessman of the duo, the one who was dependable, the one who could do the booking and who had to make apologies when Ira missed a show. By now he was a superb guitarist himself and was writing more and more songs. He was learning the music business as well, and was involved more and more in the developing music industry in Nashville. Unlike Ira's, his marriage was stable and happy, and he and Betty set about raising their children. As Ira began to make more and more threats to quit the business, Charlie began to take him more and more seriously. He was also developing more confidence in his own abilities; he was starting to feel that he could make it on his own if he had to.

Sessions 33, 34, and 35	MAY 12 AND 13, 1960
The Last Old Shovel (Jim Scott)	Cap T 1449 (LP)
Midnight Special (Traditional)	Cap T 1449 (LP)
Brown's Ferry Blues (Alton Delmore)	Cap T 1449 (LP)
Southern Moon (Alton Delmore)	Cap T 1449 (LP)
Sand Mountain Blues (Alton & Rabon Delmore)	Cap T 1449 (LP)
Nashville Blues (Alton Delmore)	Cap T 1449 (LP)
Blues Stay Away from Me (Alton Delmore-Rabon Delmore-Wayne Raney-Henry Glover)	Cap T 1449 (LP)
When It's Time for the Whippoorwill to Sing (Alton Delmore)	Cap T 1449 (LP)
Put Me on the Trail to Carolina (Alton Delmore)	Cap T 1449 (LP)
Freight Train Blues (Traditional)	Cap T 1449 (LP)
Weary Lonesome Blues (Alton Delmore)	Cap T 1449 (LP)
Gonna Lay Down My Old Guitar (Alton Delmore)	Cap T 1449 (LP)

The Louvins knew and respected many of the great duet acts of their own time, as well as many of the classic ones from the 1930s. No duet was more important to them, however, than the Delmore Brothers; like the Louvins, they came from a dirt-poor family, and like them, they had grown up in northern Alabama. As Charlie and Ira continued to celebrate their own musical heritage, it was only natural that they pay tribute to the Delmores.

The Delmores, recalls Charlie, "were without a doubt the biggest or the hottest duet that ever was on the Grand Ole Opry." The Delmores debuted on the Opry in 1933, when Ira and Charlie were still in grade school, and left the show in 1938. In between, though, they made an indelible impression on the two youngsters on Sand Mountain. As they listened for sounds they liked, sounds they could use as a model, they singled out the high harmony of the Monroe Brothers—but the smoothness of the Delmores. During their stay at the Opry, the Delmores had their hit Bluebird recordings of "Brown's Ferry Blues," "Southern Moon," "Nashville Blues," "When It's Time for the Whippoorwill to Sing," "Put Me on the Trail to Carolina," "Gonna Lay Down My Old Guitar," and "Weary Lonesome Blues"; all these they had been hearing since they were preteen boys, and all of these the Louvins recorded.

Ira and Charlie actually got to know the Delmores when they were all living in Memphis in the early 1950s. "They were working a little station up in Blytheville, Arkansas," says Charlie, "and some in West Memphis and we met 'em and knew 'em well. Alton and Rabon had the identical, the same setup as Ira and I. One teetotaller and one who couldn't stay sober." The "wild child" in the Delmore duo was the younger brother, tenor guitarist Rabon; Charlie vividly remembers one concert at which the Louvins and Delmores shared a ballpark stage with Wayne Raney and Lonnie Glosson, the harmonica players. "At the time, Arkansas was dry, and Rabon, he absolutely had to have a drink, so Ira said he'd ride with him. They went all the way back to Memphis, ten or twelve miles, to get some booze. Even with Ira drinkin' a little bit, Rabon scared him to death coming back through West Memphis at a very high rate of speed." During this time the Delmores were enjoying their "second career" with a series of rockabilly-flavored hits for King: blockbusters like "Blues Stay Away from Me," "Midnight Special," and "Freight Train Blues." It was also not far from the end of their career; by 1952 Rabon was dead from cancer, and Alton had retired back home to Alabama.

As the Louvins planned their Delmore tribute, they decided to go down to Alton's home in Huntsville. "When we went out to Alton's house, he was already in bad health." When they told him about the plans for the album, "he was beside himself. He wasn't working at all when we went out to his house. We hadn't seen him since we had met in Memphis. We were afraid we might be overlooking some song that was very big for the Delmores, and if so, show us which one it is, and sing us the tune to it. We said, 'We want to be clear on what you think is the Delmores' best.' I think the prettiest song the Delmores ever did, and we recorded it, was 'Put Me on the Trail to Carolina.' We had a list we had made that had twenty songs on it, and we had to narrow it down to a dozen; Alton took that list Ira and I had made, and looked at it. I don't know if we were lucky and actually picked the right ones, or what, but I don't think he culled any of them, saying I don't like this one better than I like that one. If he said one he liked less, we'd take it off." In a sense, then, Alton helped determine the repertoire for the album, and indirectly, the choices represent the pieces for which he felt the Delmores should best be remembered.

There was a curious footnote involving "The Midnight Special" (which the Delmores had recorded in 1945). According to Alton (when the Louvins visited him), the "midnight special" was a train that brought wives and lovers for conjugal visits at southern prisons. "The girls, they were coming," recalled Charlie, "but the prisoners didn't know who was coming, they didn't know who the midnight special was going to shine its light on." According to Alton, the brothers got the song directly from a prisoner; on one of their journeys, they had a flat tire directly in front of a prison. As the brothers changed the tire, prisoners gathered near the fence and, seeing the name "Delmore Brothers" on the side of the car, begged them to sing a few songs. Finally, after getting the tire on, they agreed to give an impromptu concert. Afterward, a black prisoner came up to the fence and told them he had written a song, and that if they could take it and do anything with it, they were welcome to. They looked at the words and saw there the version of "The Midnight Special" that they eventually sang. While there is a good chance the Delmores might have gotten their version of the song in this way, it is less likely that the prisoner composed it. The song had been recorded commercially as early as 1927, when Cryin' Sam Collins did his "Midnight Special Blues" for Gennett. In the 1930s and later, of course, Leadbelly popularized it even more.

But there was more. As Alton got more and more enthused about the project, he suddenly left the room where they were visiting. "He went under his bed and drug out this tenor guitar case, brought it into the living room, and opened it. He said, 'There's nobody touched this guitar since Rabon played it. But I'm gonna give it to you to cut this album with.' Ira had never picked a tenor guitar. And so he tuned the tenor guitar like the bottom four strings on a regular guitar; it wasn't really tuned in a tenor guitar tuning, which is somewhat different. And there were some old strings still on Rabon's guitar, and Ira took those home and took 'em off and soaked 'em in kerosene and rubbed 'em and soaked 'em in kerosene again until he got 'em alive. And he cut that album with the same strings that Rabon had played on twelve years before." (When Ira died, Charlie got the guitar back and eventually donated it to the Hall of Fame so it could be next to Alton's guitar.)

When the dates for the session rolled around, there was quite a crowd in the studio to make sure the Louvins did it right. Alton wasn't there, but Grandpa Jones and Merle Travis, old friends of the Delmores who had once joined them to form the Brown's Ferry Four and who had recorded with the Delmores for King, were there. So was Chet Atkins, primarily because of his respect for Merle and interest in what was going on. The Louvins had gotten Paul Yandell to play the guitar parts originally done by Merle in the 1940s. "Merle wanted to make sure that he played it the way Merle had played it with the Delmores," recalls Charlie. Merle had come in all the way from Los Angeles for the session, riding in a camper driven by cowboy singer Johnny Western. "Merle just laid up in the bed all the way, cause he was so weak he couldn't hardly stand up. At the session, he would watch Paul and then say, 'That's good Paul, but let me have the guitar and I'll show you the way I did it originally.' He didn't mean to make anybody mad, but he wanted to be certain it was done authentic."

Session 36 — MAY 16, 1960

It's Christmas Time (Ira and Charles Louvin)	Cap 4473
Santa's Big Parade (Ira and Charles Louvin)	Cap 4473
Love Is a Lonely Street (Ella Barrett and Faye Cunningham)	Cap 4430
If You Love Me, Stay Away (Ira and Charles Louvin)	Cap 4395

At the tail end of the Delmore Brothers session, Ira and Charlie went in to cut a throwaway Christmas single and a couple of new love songs. For the first time, they used a pedal steel on their records, played here by Pete Drake, the Nashville studio veteran. Ella Barrett, the wife of a Virginia disc jockey, collaborated with Faye Cunningham, Ira's wife, on "Love Is a Lonely Street." Drake shows to best advantage in "If You Love Me, Stay Away." "We just told him we might use the steel," says Charlie. "He just camped out on our front porch, you know, 'When's the session? Do you want to rehearse it?' And he was just there 'cause he was trying to get into the business, and we used him. I guess the first session he cut in Nashville was on that song. . . . Steel guitar is not the greatest instrument in the world when the harmonics get going. Even on duets, the way Ira and I sing, then the steel could, he's got so many variations that he can clash with harmony."

Session 37   OCTOBER 31, 1960

I Ain't Gonna Work Tomorrow (Ira and Charles Louvin)	Cap 4559
I Love You Best of All (Ira and Charles Louvin)	Cap 4506
I Can't Keep You in Love with Me (Ira and Charles Louvin)	Cap 4559
Scared of the Blues (Ira and Charles Louvin)	Cap 4506

All four of these pieces were designed for singles, and did not appear in albums until the 1964 *The Louvin Brothers Play Their Current Hits*. "I Love You Best of All" was the hit from this session, and in fact was the big Louvin hit for 1961—their first real chart success in over two years. It hit the *Billboard* list on March 19, 1961, stayed fourteen weeks, and eventually rose to no. 12. "I'm gonna admit up front that we stole that song," says Charlie. "We had sung that song all our lives. After we recorded it, nobody could find out who wrote it. We even did a copyright search—paid twenty-five dollars for it—and found the song had never been copyrighted. So we took care of that. It's a lovely, positive song."

Even though it was not in copyright, the song had been a favorite of old-time duet singers in country music in the 1920s. Mac and Bob (McFarland and Gardner), a blind duo from Knoxville who won a nationwide audience singing sentimental songs over WLS in Chicago, featured it and recorded it for the old Brunswick company in 1928. That same year another Knoxville act, Mr. and Mrs. Hugh Cross, recorded it for Columbia.

"I Ain't Gonna Work Tomorrow" is a rare instance when the Louvins added a guest star to their recording session. In this case, it was Grandpa Jones and his banjo. "That was the one he gripes so much about," laughs Charlie. "He wanted to know why it had to go to that VII chord. He had his banjo, his capo on there, and he just couldn't make that; I believe we did it in G and it'd go to F. He called it an 'off chord': 'Why do you put that off chord in there?' His clawhammer wouldn't work on that off chord good, but he wound up doing a good job on it."

Sessions 38, 39, and 40   FEBRUARY 6, 9, AND 10, 1961

I Have Found the Way (Traditional)	ST 1834 (LP)
He Set Me Free (Albert E. Brumley)	ST 1834 (LP)
Kneel at the Cross (Charles E. Moody)	ST 1834 (LP)
Leaning on the Everlasting Arms (Huffman-Showalter)	ST 1834 (LP)
O Why Not Tonight (Bonar-Bushey)	ST 1834 (LP)
You Can't Find the Lord Too Soon (Bobby Johnson)	ST 1834 (LP)
Keep Your Eyes on Jesus (Ira and Charles Louvin)	ST 1834 (LP)
Almost Persuaded (Bliss)	ST 1834 (LP)
I Feel Better Now (Ira and Charles Louvin)	ST 1834 (LP)
O Who Shall Be Able to Stand (Dale Brown)	ST 1834 (LP)
If Today Was the Day (Ira and Charles Louvin)	ST 1834 (LP)
You'll Meet Him in the Clouds [2 takes] (Ira and Charles Louvin)	unissued

In February 1961, at the dawn of the Kennedy era, the brothers began work on their fourth all-gospel album, *Keep Your Eyes on Jesus*. It was to be their first stereo album, and possibly for that reason Ken Nelson decided to enhance the basic Louvin sound that had served him so well for the past five years. Added to the Jimmy Capps-Ray Edenton team was piano player Marvin Hughes, who had played on the "Love Thy Neighbor" session back in 1955. "Marvin worked for Acuff-Rose as a scorer," recalled Charlie. It was his job to make lead sheets from tapes so the company could send them for copyright. Later he became an A & R (Artists and Repertoire) man for Capitol. His romping, gospel quartet-style piano added a lot to the fills and turnarounds on the new numbers. Then, for one of the three sessions (that of February 9, which yielded "O Why Not Tonight"), Nelson added the famed Jordanaires to do backup vocals. Known for their work with Elvis as well as their own records for Capitol, the group gave the four numbers from February 9 a distinct gospel quartet feeling. To top off the experiments at this one day's session, Nelson added a set of vibes, possibly played by Owen Bradley, about the only vibe player in town then. The other sessions—the first and third—featured the more traditional Louvin sound, with Hughes's piano added.

The album was a random mixture of old gospel songs, nineteenth century hymns, originals, and modern gospel efforts. "I Have Found the Way," though listed as "traditional," was in fact written by Rev. L. A. Green and arranger Adger Pace and dated from the 1940s; Pace was the music editor for the James D. Vaughan Company, a pioneer in shape-note songbooks. "He Set Me Free" is an Albert E. Brumley song that was popularized by the Chuck Wagon Gang in the 1940s. It first appeared in a 1939 Stamps-Baxter songbook called *Gospel Tide* and is best known as the model on which Hank Williams built "I Saw the Light." "Kneel at the Cross" was the masterpiece of Charles E. Moody, the Georgia songwriter who moonlighted as a member of the best-selling old-time string band the Georgia Yellow Hammers. "Leaning on the Everlasting Arms," a church standard, was by Elisha A. Huffman and A. J. Showalter, and was first published by Showalter's music company in a book called *The Glad Evangel* in 1887.

"O Why Not Tonight" is another nineteenth-century gospel hymn, one that dates in part as far back as 1842; Ira adds to it an original narrative in front of an organ-piano backing. In "You Can't Find the Lord too Soon" Ira does a sort of chanted sermon in front of the quartet's smooth drive, sort of a gospel patter song. "Keep Your Eyes on Jesus," an original, features an easy lope and deft interplay between the brothers and the Jordanaires. The venerable "Almost Persuaded" spotlights Charlie's solo, framed by the discrete vibraphone.

The last session had even more of an old-time quartet feeling, even though the Jordanaires were absent. Ira lead "I Feel Better Now," with Hughes piano prominent. Ira's mandolin is featured on "O Who Shall Be Able to Stand" and "If Today Was the Day." "You'll Meet Him in the Clouds," which seems to have given the singers some trouble, resembles the verse to the standard "If I Could Hear My Mother Pray Again," and offers another impressive piano break.

The experiment with the Jordanaires satisfied both Nelson and the Louvins, and three months later they used the Jordanaires again on a Christmas album.

Sessions 41, 42, and 43	MAY 10, 11, AND 12, 1961
Away in a Manger	ST 1616 (LP)
The Friendly Beasts	ST 1616 (LP)
Hark the Herald Angels Sing	ST 1616 (LP)
Good Christian Men Rejoice	ST 1616 (LP)
While the Shepherds Watched Their Flocks	ST 1616 (LP)
The First Noel	ST 1616 (LP)
It Came upon a Midnight Clear	ST 1616 (LP)

O Come All You Faithful	ST 1616 (LP)
O Little Town of Bethlehem	ST 1616 (LP)
Silent Night	ST 1616 (LP)
Deck the Halls	ST 1616 (LP)
Joy to the World	ST 1616 (LP)

"That's the hardest album we ever cut," recalls Charlie. "But I think it was one of the best. I don't like to brag, but it was as good as anything that Tennessee Ernie Ford ever cut." Louvin purists have complained about the decision to add voices to the orignal duet sound here, but the brothers were both happy about it. The voices were not overdubbed later but done "live" in the Nashville studios by no less a group than the Jordanaires. For the first time, the Louvins had to contend with formal notions of harmony and part singing. "Gordon Stoker [of the Jordanaires] taught Ira and I the parts. You think you know songs and sing them all your life, but when you get in the studio to cut 'em, there's just little quirks and bends there that you never dreamed of. We'd sing a song and Gordon would come over and say, 'This tenor right here that you're doing—that's not a tenor, that's a solo part.' Gordon would show Ira what a true tenor was. We were good at seconding the voices to both of us. If we'd done it as a duet, we'd sing it quite different than it came off with the Jordanaires."

In spite of the hard work and the satisfaction the brothers got from the album (finally titled *Christmas with the Louvin Brothers*), Capitol only kept it on the market two years and then deleted it. It remains today one of the rarest and most sought-after Louvin LPs.

Session 44   MAY 13, 1961

It Hurts Me More (The Second Time Around) (Bill Anderson)	Cap 4628
How's the World Treating You (Chet Atkins-Boudleaux Bryant)	Cap 4628
Every Time You Leave (Ira and Charles Louvin)	Cap 5075
Time Goes So Slow (Marie Wilson-Skeeter Davis)	Cap 4757

"Every Time You Leave" is a Louvin song that Charlie still sings today and one that he included in the 1990 *Now, Then, and Forever* album. "If you listen to the song—regardless of what Ira would say to one of his wives, I hate to say which one, she'd just leave. It was like an every other week thing. But he'd say, 'Well, she'll be back.' And he eventually wrote a song about it. She always did come back. He'd do anything to get her to come back. When a man gets in that position, where he says, 'You can do anything and I'll take you back,' you're gonna be hurting."

"How's the World Treating You?" charted briefly in October 1961, peaking at no. 26. It bore composer credits by Chet Atkins and "Rocky Top" master Boudleaux Bryant. "All I can tell you is that it's a good song," recalls Charlie.

Sessions 45, 46, and 47   JULY 25, 26, AND 27, 1961

I Died for the Red White and Blue	Cap ST 1721 (LP)
From Mother's Arms to Korea (C & I Louvin)	Cap ST 1721 (LP)
Searching for a Soldier's Grave (Roy Acuff)	Cap ST 1721 (LP)
At Mail Call Today (Fred Rose-Gene Autry)	Cap ST 1721 (LP)
A Soldier's Last Letter (Ernest Tubb-Henry Stewart)	Cap ST 1721 (LP)
There's a Star-Spangled Banner Waving Somewhere (Roberts-Darnell)	Cap ST 1721 (LP)
There's a Grave in the Wave of the Ocean (Grandpa Jones)	Cap ST 1721 (LP)
Mother I Thank for the Bible You Gave (Traditional)	Cap ST 1721 (LP)
The Great Atomic Power (C & I Louvin-Buddy Bain)	Cap ST 1721 (LP)
A Seaman's Girl (Ella Barrett-Faye Cunningham)	Cap ST 1721 (LP)
Robe of White (I & C Louvin)	Cap ST 1721 (LP)
The Weapon of Prayer (I & C Louvin)	Cap 4686
Broken Engagement (Charles and Ira Louvin)	Cap 4757

In late July 1961 the brothers began work on what would be *The Weapon of Prayer* album. It was designed from the start as an album, and only one single was ever pulled from it; the balance of the songs were issued only in the form of Capitol ST 1721. Although John F. Kennedy had been inaugurated as president in January, the military situation was tense and the fear of war was in the air; the U.S. had broken off diplomatic relations with Cuba, and in April the CIA had joined Cuban nationals in the Bay of Pigs fiasco. Still, the immediate impetus for an album of war songs was a picture. "Did you see the cover of that?" asks Charlie. "Ken Veeder, who was one of Capitol's best photographers, took a lot of pictures of the Louvin Brothers. He was somewhere in Pennsylvania, and this boy left for the army, and they gave him this picture. 'Cause Ken was always hunting for something that would make an album cover. Ken Nelson thought this was the greatest picture he ever saw in his life, this boy standing at the train, with his bags packed, in a uniform. He said, 'Let's cut an album. I want to cut an album, I want to use this picture. Come up with an album so I can use this picture.' So the first one we thought of was "The Weapon of Prayer." Then we remembered, we had really slayed them during the big war with all these war songs. I said, 'Hell, we can put an album like that together, Ken.' And he said, 'Put it together.' So we just gathered up all these songs."

They added Grandpa Jones's old World War II hit "There's a Grave in the Wave of the Ocean," and the brothers' own 1952 hit "The Great Atomic Power." There was "A Seaman's Girl," a new song written by Ira's wife Faye along with her Virginia friend Ella Barrett. "It was actually Ella's song; Ira smoothed it out a little bit and took half of it for Faye. He pulled a Webb Pierce right there." (Pierce was noted for cutting himself in as co-composer for songs he recorded.) "Robe of White" dated from the brothers' MGM days, as did "Weapon of Prayer." "At Mail Call Today" had been a hit by both Gene Autry and Red Foley back in 1945, and "Soldier's Last Letter" had been Ernest Tubb's second chart hit back in 1944. The set was rounded out by other familiar country and gospel songs, mostly from the 1940s.

Session 48   MAY 9, 1962

The First Time in Life (Ira and Charles Louvin)	Cap 4822
There Is No Easy Way (Ira and Charles Louvin)	Cap 5075
Love Turned to Hate (Skeeter Davis)	Cap 4941
Must You Throw Dirt in My Face? (Bill Anderson)	Cap 4822

"Must You Throw Dirt in My Face?" was the most successful song from this session, and in fact became the last single the brothers saw hit the charts. In November 1962, it spent six weeks there, moving up to no. 21. It was an early effort by Bill Anderson, who by now had already started his own recording career. "I never will forget the first time I heard that song," says Charlie. "Went to Bill Anderson's office to hear that. He was sure that he had a Louvin Brothers song. I had a copy of the lyrics, and Ira had a copy; Bill played it on a tape. By the time the song was finished, I could have took my lyrics and rolled them up into a ball this big. That song just fractured me. I never led that kind of life, but I like that kind of song."

Another unusual item from the session was "The First Time in Life," on which the label credits mention "The Slater Sisters" as assisting on the chorus. This was simply Ira's wife Faye and two of the Louvin sisters, Ailene and Lorene. "That song will knock your hat in a creek," muses Charlie. "The song demanded a boy-girl arrangement; rather than just use the one girl, we used harmony parts."

TWO DIFFERENT WORLDS

The end began in an odd and inauspicious way. In the fall of 1962, on November 17, the Louvins' "Must You Throw Dirt in My Face?" entered the *Billboard* charts. It wasn't to be a major hit, spending only six weeks on the charts and never rising above no. 21. It was, however, to be the last Louvin Brothers single to make the charts, and it was symptomatic of the quiet way in which their career would end—not with a bang, indeed, but with a whimper.

By this time, too, a man named Paul Wyatt had come into Nashville to be the new on-the-scene producer for Capitol's increasingly busy country schedule. As Charlie remembers: "Ken Nelson never did want a Capitol office in this town. He would fly in from California, stay up here two or three weeks, cut everybody, and go back home. But the office here eventually happened anyway. They got Paul Wyatt, who was a pretty good producer. And he said to Ira and I one day, 'What do you think about Roy Acuff?' And we said we loved Acuff, that we were raised on Acuff. And he said, 'Why don't you pick out twelve of your favorites and let's do a tribute to Roy Acuff.' That pleased us to death, and it took us about two days to put the list together."

Wyatt looked over the song list and approved it. As with the Delmore Brothers tribute album, the Louvins wanted to get some input from the people they were honoring. In this case, they decided to use some of Roy Acuff's regular band members to play on the session: Pete Kirby (Bashful Brother Oswald) on dobro, Howdy Forrester on fiddle, Jimmie Riddle on harmonica and piano, and Shot Jackson on steel. Wyatt worked out a budget for the sessions and, as he was required to do, sent it to Capitol headquarters on the coast for approval. There it ran into problems; it came across Ken Nelson's desk and Nelson told Wyatt, "I think it's a bad idea. I don't want it done." Wyatt was stunned; he was convinced that the album was an excellent idea, and the more

On Sand Mountain

he planned it, the more excited he became. He took the unheard-of step of
going over Nelson's head. Charlie recalls: "He showed it to the big wigs. They
said, 'It's a great idea. We don't care what the budget is, let's do it.'"

Unbeknownst to the Nashville group at the time, however, Nelson had some
privileged information. He was an early influential officer in the Country Music

Association, the trade organization that elects stars to the Hall of Fame. Charlie believes that Nelson had advance information that 1962's honoree would be Acuff. (He was, in fact, that year's honoree and became the first living artist elected to the Hall of Fame.) In anticipation of that event, Nelson was readying a "greatest hits" reissue of some of Acuff's best Capitol sides; he hoped to take advantage of the publicity surrounding Acuff's election to the Hall of Fame. The album soon came out. As Nelson explained it later to Charlie, "I already had all of those songs [i.e., the ones the Louvins wanted to record] picked to go into this Hall of Fame album. Why should the Louvin Brothers come out with the same songs bucking another Capitol album?"

But Wyatt had already gotten his permission to go ahead with the project, and went into Sam Phillips's recording studio on Seventh Avenue North in Nashville with Charlie and Ira. There, on two all-day sessions on June 21 and 22, 1962, they cut the twelve songs for the tribute album.

Sessions 49 and 50   NASHVILLE JUNE 21 AND 22, 1962

The Great Speckled Bird (Traditional)	Cap ST 2827 (LP)
Wabash Cannonball (William Kindt)	Cap ST 2827 (LP)
Lonely Mound of Clay (Roy Acuff)	Cap ST 2827 (LP)
Wreck on the Highway (Dorsey Dixon)	Cap ST 2827 (LP)
Wait for the Light to Shine (Fred Rose)	Cap ST 2827 (LP)
Low and Lonely (Floyd Jenkins)	Cap ST 2827 (LP)
We Live in Two Different Worlds (Fred Rose)	Cap ST 2827 (LP)
The Precious Jewel (Roy Acuff)	Cap ST 2827 (LP)
The Great Judgment Morning (Traditional)	Cap ST 2827 (LP)
Branded Wherever I Go (Roy Acuff)	Cap ST 2827 (LP)
Not a Word from Home (Roy Acuff)	Cap ST 2827 (LP)
Stuck Up Blues (Roy Acuff)	Cap ST 2827 (LP)

To augment the Acuff backup men, the Louvins got well-known singer Cowboy Copas to add his unique flattop guitar sound to the whole session. With such a wealth of studio talent, neither Louvin played guitar or mandolin—one of the first times that had ever happened. Studio regular Ray Edenton played rhythm and Junior Huskey played bass.

The songs themselves were all Acuff standards, and several of them were such standards that any Acuff album would have to include them. But beyond these standards, the Louvins chose songs that best reflected their own aesthetic, and these deserve comment. "The Great Judgement Morning" dates back to 1941, when the Louvins were just starting their own career and watching Acuff at local schoolhouse shows. Though generally listed as "Public Domain" or "Traditional," it had been written in the 1930s by Rev. Burt Shaddock and one L. L. Picke. It was one of several early Acuff gospel songs that had come from the old shape-note songbooks, especially those of publisher R. E. Winsett of Dayton, Tennessee. "Stuck Up Blues" also was first recorded by Acuff back in 1941; though it bears Acuff's name, he had in fact purchased it from well-known Nashville songwriter Jim Anglin, who had provided so much material for Johnnie and Jack. Another Anglin song was "Lonely Mound of Clay," purchased by Acuff a few months before he had recorded it in 1940. Though sometimes associated with World War II, in fact the song had arisen from an incident that occurred in Anglin's hometown in Alabama. A neighbor had had to leave home to look for work during the Depression, and when he returned he found that his wife had passed away. Both in its sentiment and its Alabama ties (Anglin had grown up in Athens, Alabama, near Sand Mountain), it had a special appeal to the Louvins. Several other songs from the session came from the brothers' old publisher and mentor, Fred Rose (including one under his pseudonym, Floyd Jenkins). "Branded Wherever I Go," with its theme of persecution, had obvious appeal for Ira, while "Not a Word from Home" had the kind of domestic appeal seen in so many of the Louvins' own songs.

The album was soon completed, and the Louvins left the studio satisfied they had done a good piece of work. But the story was not finished. Wyatt's attempt to go over Nelson's head eventually cost him his job at Capitol-Nashville; and, out of anger, Nelson refused to release the album. Even after Acuff's own Capitol reissue set had come out and sold its course, the master tapes for the Louvin tribute sat on the shelf. It was a whole five years before the recording was finally issued, and then under conditions no one possibly could have foreseen.

Session 51   NOVEMBER 1, 1962

Don't Let Them Take the Bible Out of Our School	
Rooms (G. D McGray)	Cap 4886
I'm Glad That I'm Not Him (Ira and Charles Louvin)	Cap 4999
A Message to Your Heart (Ira and Charles Louvin)	Cap 4999

The last non-gospel session for the brothers was an odd three-song affair in November 1962 in the midst of the fight about the Acuff album. The main reason for the session was a topical song that Nelson wanted to rush out,

"Don't Let Them Take the Bible Out of Our School Rooms." The author, G. D. McGray was from Virginia. "He sent us the song and we liked what it said, and so we presented it to Nelson. And because the school prayer thing was in the courts at that time, he thought that it would play; and it did play, quite well. Some of them were quite emphatic about why this law should not be, and if they could be around today to see what's happened to the youth, they'd have been more emphatic."

"A Message to Your Heart" grew from a title that Ira came up with. "He was trying to do some things with his women and wasn't getting much response. So he felt like they might hear it more in his music than saying it with a pencil. That song is widely used in the bluegrass field now."

The inevitable breakup finally came in August 1963, and it was neither especially dramatic nor overly acrimonious. It seems to have started at a concert tour date with Ray Price in Watsexa, Illinois. The morning after the show, it was raining and Ira woke up in a bad mood; he accused Charlie of moving his mandolin. "Don't ever touch it again," he shouted. "And when we finish this date and get home, you can hang it up, because this is absolutely my last date." Charlie replied, "Well, I've heard that more than a hundred times, I know, but you've never heard that from me. I've been trying to hold this thing together, but I agree now! It's true—this *is* the last date we'll play together." They picked up their pay (two hundred and fifty dollars, one of the lowest fees they'd gotten in years) and drove back to Nashville.

Charlie and Betty decided to take some time off; they drove the Loudermilk parents to Florida, visited the Smokies, and generally relaxed and visited. On the way back to Nashville one Saturday night they began listening to the Opry. They heard Roy Acuff come on and say, "Ira Louvin is here with us tonight and is gonna help us sing this song." With this, Charlie began to sense that the break was really complete. He had already talked to Ken Nelson about staying on Capitol as a soloist, and had already talked to the Opry bosses as well.

The next Friday Ira called Charlie as if nothing had ever happened and asked, "What time are we on the Opry?" Charlie said, "We're not on. I'm on at such and such a time." There was a long silence on the phone, and then Ira got angry. After listening to shouts for several minutes, Charlie said, "I just took you at your word, but you remember what I told you."

They had had a new gospel album scheduled for recording in early September; the studio had been booked, the musicians contracted, and the songs selected. The brothers had even been rehearsing the new numbers. In spite of the harsh words and breakup, both agreed that it made sense to go ahead and record it; they owed Ken Nelson that much for all his help in the past. No one, not even the Opry managers, were sure that the Louvin split was permanent; Nelson wasn't sure either, but sensed that neither Louvin on his own would do as well as the duo. If a final gospel album might help keep the act afloat, he too was all for it.

Sessions 52, 53, and 54   SEPTEMBER 11 AND 12, 1963

Thank God for My Christian Home (Ira Louvin-Anne Young)	Cap ST 2331 (LP)
I'll Never Die (Ira Louvin-Anne Young)	Cap ST 2331 (LP)
The Price on the Bottle (Ira Louvin-Anne Young)	Cap ST 2331 (LP)
I've Known a Lady (Ira and Charles Louvin)	Cap ST 2331 (LP)
He Included Me (Ira Louvin)	Cap ST 2331 (LP)
Keep Watching the Sky (Ira Louvin)	Cap ST 2331 (LP)
How Lord, What Can I Do for You (Ira Louvin-Anne Young)	Cap ST 2331 (LP)
Way Upon a Mountain (Ira Louvin-Anne Young)	Cap ST 2331 (LP)
Gonna Shake Hands With Mother over There (Ira and Charles Louvin)	
He Was Waiting at the Altar (Ira Louvin-Anne Young)	Cap ST 2331 (LP)
Oh Lord, My God (Tommy Hagen)	Cap ST 2331 (LP)
What Would You Take in Exchange for My Soul? (J. J. Berry-J. H. Carr)	Cap ST 2331 (LP)

The last Louvin Brothers album became *Thank God for My Christian Home*. The album was done, technically speaking, after the brothers had broken up in August. "We had this album prepared, the budget was in, and although we was busted up, why not go ahead and cut it? So we did." Charlie wanted Ira to give him permission to continue to use the name "The Louvins" in the music business, and to that end had struck a deal whereby he took his name off some three hundred songs that he and Ira held jointly. The plan didn't work out, but in the meantime Ira added his new wife's name, Anne Young, to some of the pieces in this last session.

In spite of their troubles, the brothers still managed to create some masterpieces in this last session. The recitation on "The Price on the Bottle" was based on a true incident in which Ira had gone to a package store and watched a boy buying a bottle. "I've Known a Lady" is the song Charlie today calls "my all-time favorite," and one he recently included in his album *And That's the Gospel.* "It was as effective as anything Ira ever did," he says.

"Oh Lord, My God" looked to the future; it was penned by Tommy Hagen, the singer Charlie had found to replace Ira as tenor in his new act. Hagen was in the studio for this session, watching Ira and learning the style firsthand. He later sang Ira's parts on Charlie's first solo album.

The last song cut, symbolically, looked back toward the past, when the brothers were fresh from Sand Mountain and just beginning the long, strange road that was to lead them to this moment. "What Would You Take in Exchange for My Soul?" was the first great song from the Monroe Brothers, who had recorded it some twenty-seven years earlier. It became an anthem for them and a standard for all those who came after. For the Louvins, it was a most appropriate swan song.

Ira wanted out of the increasingly hectic Nashville scene. His plan was to retire to Sand Mountain and start some kind of little business. Ken Nelson, in fact, loaned him some money to set up what Nelson described as a "workshop." He had married again, this time to Anne Young, a Canadian singer who was known for her yodeling and who had been performing on minor league Nashville radio in the 1950s.

He seemed determined to simplify his life. He gave away his white silk suits and settled in. Charlie came down and helped him build a Jim Walters prefabricated home, and the two brothers decided to start their own music publishing company, C & I. (It stood, of course, for Charlie and Ira, and Ira drew up a logo for it—a big eyeball, as in "Seeing Eye.") Ira had by now also become an expert instrument repairman; even before the split, he had started working at Shot Jackson's Sho-Bud shop in Nashville. Among his creations there was an odd five-string electric mandolin that he actually used on a couple of records and for which he later filed a patent. He also completed a prototype for a new style electric Spanish guitar, made of bird's-eye maple with pearl inlay. Most unusual of all his experiments, though, was a little "high G" guitar; this was a six-string guitar, blonde with a black single electric pickup, but not much bigger than a mandolin. It was completed in 1964 and appeared on the cover of Ira's first and only solo album for Capitol, *The Unforgettable Ira Louvin.* He supposedly played the little instrument on his last show date, in Kansas City. As far as can be determined, none of these instruments actually went into production, but they reveal the kind of direction Ira was going in during his last days. His creativity was undiminished, but was taking new and equally frustrating forms.

In spite of his resolution, Ira couldn't stay away from the music business. He began working on a solo album, as did Charlie. At first, both showed renewed success with singles from these albums. Ira had a couple of single issues, one of which was "Yodel, Sweet Molly," which spent four weeks on the charts in 1965. Charlie had his first solo hit in June 1964 with a fine new Bill Anderson song, "I Don't Like You Anymore." For it Charlie recruited Tommy Hagen, the North Carolina singer who had worked with Jimmy Capps, to sing Ira's part in the new records he was doing.

Charlie also talked to Ira about getting the rights to use the name "The Louvins" in his act, but decided against it; he determined to forge his own career, one based on Charlie Louvin songs, not Louvin Brothers nostalgia. Ken Nelson was still not sure about the breakup, but reluctantly approved development of solo albums by each brother.

In the summer of 1964 came an odd event that bothered Charlie and seemed to hint at the tragedy that was just around the corner. Charlie was working on Ernest Tubb's "Midnight Jamboree," the late-night show that came on in the wee hours of the morning after the Opry had signed off. It was held in Ernest Tubb's old record shop in Lower Broadway in Nashville. Bill Monroe and his group were doing the show, and Ira unexpectedly showed up. "He just happened to be in town," recalled Charlie. "We talked him into doing a number, and he borrowed Bill Monroe's mandolin. Bill doesn't let many people touch that mandolin, much less borrow it. But Bill liked Ira and he let Ira use it." Afterwards, the group retired down the street to Linebaugh's, the old restaurant that for years had been the gathering place for musicians. Ira returned Monroe's mandolin, and Bill asked, "What'd you play?" Ira told him, and they all talked for a few minutes. Charlie recalls: "Then Ira told Bill, 'I want you to sing "Swing Low, Sweet Chariot" at my funeral.' Bill, trying to kid Ira, answered, 'Okay, but I want you to sing at my funeral.'" It was a friendly pact, but it made everyone a bit uneasy.

In the summer of 1965, Ira and Anne were working as a duo, doing some songwriting, and spending a lot of their time at their home in Henagar. In June Ira got a booking for a couple of shows in Missouri—one at the old Chesnut Club near Kansas City, and others at New Bloomfield and Jefferson City, near the center of the state. He and Anne decided to drive up with Billy and Adelle

Barksdale, friends from nearby Ft. Payne, Alabama; the Barksdales were not especially musicians, but Mr. Barksdale was the owner of the Coca-Cola bottling company in Ft. Payne. The Barksdales could help while away the time on the long drive and help with the driving.

The pair did all the shows and early Sunday morning, June 20, headed home to Henagar. They were traveling west on a recently opened section of new Interstate 70 near Williamsburg, in Calaway County, Missouri. Even today, no one knows exactly what happened, but there was a grinding crash and a head-on collision. The other car was coming from St. Louis and began skidding in the oncoming side of the interstate; both cars, according to troopers, were traveling at a high rate of speed.

When the first troopers arrived on the scene, they found five bodies: Ira, the Barksdales, and two men from the other car. Anne was still alive and was rushed to the hospital at Fulton, and then to the University of Missouri Medical Center at Columbia; there she was pronounced dead on arrival. As officers photographed and measured the wreck site, they found in the St. Louis car five opened pints of liquor, as well as several cans of beer.

Charlie learned the news later that afternoon in West Virginia. "I had played the Saturday night before in Asheville and drove straight through for a date in Culpepper, West Virginia. I had only slept three or four hours, and I hadn't had the radio on, so I hadn't heard anything. I pulled into the music park at about one o'clock that afternoon, and I was due for a show at two. I was met at the gate by Sonny James, who just told me I had to call home at once. I had to drive two or three miles back down the road to get to the nearest phone, but I found one and called home. My wife told me what had happened. They had gotten her out of church for it that morning."

Charlie returned to the music park and debated what to do. The word had spread through the crowd, and they were talking in subdued tones. "I told the disc jockey doing the announcing not to say anything about it," says Charlie. "I went ahead and did the 2:00 PM show and then another show that night. I figured I had driven all that distance to do the show and the people were expecting me. And there wasn't a thing I could do for anyone. It would be a day and a half before my brother's body came to Nashville, and I couldn't see going into mourning. I didn't do it because the show had to go on. I did it because there was nothing else I could do. The next morning I caught a 10:00 AM flight from Washington. I didn't do any Louvin Brothers songs on the show like I normally would have done, because I knew I couldn't have got through them. I wasn't that brave."

LEGACY

As it turned out, Bill Monroe kept his word. He was working in Pennsylvania when he learned that Ira had died. He dropped his entire schedule, returned to Nashville, and sang at the funeral, as he had promised. It was a couple of years later that he made his final assessment of Ira. When a reporter asked him about the history of tenor singers in country music, he responded, "Ain't but two, and Ira's dead."

In addition to Charlie, Ira was survived by his parents, by his son Terry (then only twelve), and by two daughters, Gail (then 24) and Kathy Faye (then only seven). There were five sisters, most still living on Sand Mountain. Though it seemed as if Ira had been in the business forever, he was actually only forty-one.

As friends and business associates and music industry figures gathered at the Phillips-Robinson Funeral Home to pay their respects, there was still a sense of shock at the suddenness of it all. There was a lot of talk about the country music "curse"—about the unbelievable string of deaths that had dogged the industry in the two preceding years. Patsy Cline, Cowboy Copas, Hawkshaw Hawkins, Randy Hughes, Jack Anglin, Texas Ruby, Jim Reeves, and Dean Manuel all had died in tragic accidents in recent months. It was almost as if an entire generation of country music was being wiped out. An even crueler irony was that officials got the remains of Anne Young and Mrs. Barksdale confused; Anne had let her friend wear a special ring she had, and that ring was one of the few ways of identifying the bodies. As a result, Anne's body was mistakenly sent to Ft. Payne and Mrs. Barksdale's to Nashville.

During their thirteen-year recording career, from 1947 through 1963, the Louvins saw their music appear in just about every recorded form, from the old fragile 78s to the 45s, EPs, radio transcriptions, tape, demo disc, and LP. They left a body of some 219 commercially recorded songs and a series of eighteen

LP albums done for Capitol. (Few of them were in print at the time Ira died.) Charlie estimates that the duo wrote some four hundred songs, spread out over three publishing companies, and that over the years they garnered some eighteen songwriting awards. Both have been inducted into the Songwriters Hall of Fame.

The week of the funeral, Charlie was watching his third solo hit, "See the Big Man Cry," climb the *Billboard* charts. A year earlier, in June 1964, he had made his first solo recordings, with a release he felt good about called "Book of Memories." It was a Louvin-style duet with Tommy Hagen singing Ira's part. To back it up on the single, they had decided on a Bill Anderson song called "I Don't Love You Anymore." "We had about five minutes left in the recording session, when we decided to record the song," remembers Charlie. "So within five minutes, we put down the cut that was released. Bill Grammar dreamed up the guitar run that's in it. The song eventually stayed on the charts for twenty-six weeks. I'd have to credit Bill Anderson with establishing my individual career." To his surprise, the hit of the pairing was not a Louvin-style duet but a Charlie Louvin solo. The ones that followed, "Less and Less" (December 1965) and "See the Big Man Cry" were also strict solos—no harmony on the refrain, and not even any background singers humming along.

By the time Ira died, in short, Charlie was not just fumbling around toward a solo career; he was well established and was one of the hotter singers around. His albums, which began to appear at regular intervals, often at first contained several Louvin Brothers songs, though more often than not done solo style. Increasingly, though, Charlie began drawing from the commercial Nashville songwriting establishment, which he knew well. He became one of the first major artists to record songs by the writers who would change the face of country music songwriting in the 1960s. These included Bill Anderson, Ed Bruce (who wrote "See the Big Man Cry"), young Roger Miller ("Less and Less"), Willie Nelson ("I Just Don't Understand"), Johnny Russell ("Making Plans"), and Kris Kristofferson ("The Perfect Stranger"). Charlie found a new songwriting partner in Larry Lee, and began to add his own songs to the collections.

All in all, Charlie had twenty singles between 1964 and 1972 that sold well enough to win a place on the *Billboard* charts; ironically, this is more hits than the Louvins themselves had had during their heyday. Eventually Charlie's solo work would encompass twenty-two albums on three labels, as well as 101 singles. With his own distinctive "low" tenor, he soon developed a familiar country style of his own and soon had enough major hits to fill out a lengthy stage show. But onstage, Charlie generally kept a segment in the show in which he played tribute to the Louvin sound. Over the years, numerous singers have sung Ira's part in this segment: Tommy Hagen, bass player Rex Ellis, veteran bluegrass star Monroe Fields, and Louisiana singer Charles Whitstein.

Harmony, even if not the Ira and Charlie variety, has continued to be a part of Charlie's music. The high, clean harmonies (essentially two tenors) that marked the Louvin style began to lose favor in the country music world of the 1960s and 1970s. In its place was a trend for male-female duets, first popularized in the 1940s by husband and wife teams like Lulu Belle and Scotty and Wilma Lee and Stoney Cooper. Starting in the 1960s teams like Carl and Pearl Butler ("Don't Let Me Cross Over"), David Houston and Tammy Wynette ("My Elusive Dreams"), and Conway Twitty and Loretta Lynn began to place duets again on the hit charts—though they were seldom in the close harmony style of the Louvin Brothers.

Charlie easily adapted to this new manner of harmony singing. His first partner was a young woman named Dianne McCall. "Dianne was with me from 1969 to 1974. I met her in Illinois and hired her because I was going to Las Vegas. I decided to add something to my show for people to look at as well as listen to." Starting in 1970, he replaced Dianne with a better known singer, Melba Montgomery. She had learned her singing in the rural Methodist church around Florence, Alabama, where she grew up. Her strong, husky style soon won her a place in Roy Acuff's troupe, and in 1962 her record company teamed her with George Jones. A series of hits followed—the best known being Melba's own composition, "We Must Have Been Out of Our Minds"—and by 1969 she found herself on the same label as Charlie, Capitol. During the following three years, she and Charlie got together on a number of singles and albums, reviving some of the old gospel harmony. Their big hits included "Something to Brag About" (1970) and "Did You Ever" (1971). "We should have done more ballads," Charlie laments in retrospect. "We let them talk us into doing too many novelty things."

Through the 1970s, Charlie moved into even more modern country ar-rangements. He left his longtime home at Capitol in 1973 and moved to United Artists, where he continued to produce marketable Top 40 fare like "You're My Wife, She's My Woman" (1974). Although he was becoming known as one of the best businessmen in the Nashville music scene and one of the best judges of new songs, and although he could keep up with the slickest of the new sounds, he continued to keep alive the old Louvin fire. He still lived at Henagar, and started his own festival there, May on the Mountain, which focused on traditional country music and bluegrass. He opened a Louvin Brothers museum, full of his old pictures and songbooks and artifacts. He also greeted the younger musicians, the ones they were beginning to call bluegrass or new traditionalists, and told them about the Louvins. He found old Louvin songs that Ira had been working on and resurrected them for a new generation. He even recorded a duet with Emmylou Harris ("Love Don't Care"), and a trio with bluegrass stars Jim and Jesse ("North Wind"). In 1992 he joined forces with tenor singer Charles Whitstein and began a series of tours called The Louvin Brothers Music Celebration. It featured Louvin songs almost exclusively and attracted new fans, huge crowds, overseas tours, and led to a new album.

In the meantime, the Louvin songs and the Louvin style were continuing to impact American music on a number of fronts. The first of these was bluegrass; during the late 1960s and early 1970s, as the slick "countrypolitan" sound and the urban cowboy movement swept mainstream country, the young bluegrass and folk-rock bands were discovering just how hard it was to do good harmony singing.

Jim and Jesse, old friends of the Louvins, turned a half dozen Louvin songs into bluegrass standards, including "Are You Missing Me," which they had recorded at the dawn of their career in 1952. In later years, as Jim and Jesse emerged as a major bluegrass act on the Grand Ole Opry, they continued to feature Louvin songs, even to the point of doing an entire album in tribute to them on a national label in 1969. The Osborne Brothers, another pioneering bluegrass act, took the Louvin song "A Message to Your Heart" and made it into a favorite; Bobby Osborne, the mandolin player of the team, occasionally worked up Louvin Brothers duets with Charlie on the Opry shows. More modern groups, such as the Washington, D.C.-based Country Gentlemen, adapted Louvin songs like "Love and Wealth" to increasingly complex three- and four-part harmonies. Joe Val, New England's leading bluegrass singer, kept Louvin songs in his repertoire and on his albums as he played in Boston and New England. The Pinnacle Boys, the Allen Brothers, Carl Story, the Johnson Mountain Boys, the Shenandoah Cut-Ups, Reno and Harrell, Del McCoury, the Lewis Family, Mac Wiseman, the Crowe Brothers, Red Allen, the Nashville Bluegrass Band, the Stanley Brothers, the Doug Dillard Band, Hylo Brown, the Bluegrass Cardinals, Doyle Lawson and Quicksilver, and others have all recorded Louvin songs. Flatt and Scruggs, before their breakup in 1969, had recorded numerous Louvin songs, and after the split Lester Flatt devoted a portion of his bluegrass festival to a special Louvin tribute.

For many years, the mainstream country act that best featured Louvin songs was the Browns, best known for hits like "The Three Bells." Their first chart hit was a lovely reading of the Louvins' "I Take the Chance," and through a long series of later albums they lent their mellow three-part harmony to dozens of Louvin songs, keeping them alive for folk as well as country fans. Honky-tonk singer Carl Smith and the duo of Johnnie and Jack had made Louvin songs a part of their careers early on, and Smith's version of "Are You Teasing Me" was one of his first big hits. Soloists such as Don Gibson, Roy Acuff, Jean Shepherd, and Kitty Wells all did Louvin songs, while more modern harmony groups like the Kendalls redid Louvin favorites. Jumpin' Bill Carlisle and his family group the Carlisles kept alive on the Opry stage the bizarre novelty songs Ira liked to do, and were still singing "On the Way to the Show" and "Is Zat You Myrtle" in 1995. Fans of the rock pioneers the Everly Brothers have noted that, in the words of Alan Cackett, the Everly style "could best be described as the Louvin Brothers polished and commercialized for the urban market."

The emergence of the so-called "new traditionalism" in the 1980s brought back into vogue the high, classic close harmony style, and singers like Randy Travis, Vince Gill, Ricky Skaggs, the Whites, and many of the younger stars found themselves looking to the Louvin music for inspiration. It no longer embarrassed anybody to hear adjectives like "the greatest" used about the Louvins. In 1995, Marty Stuart, who was becoming a spokesman for the new generation's respect for tradition, said: "Without a doubt, Charlie and Ira Louvin were one of the greatest duos in country music. The songs and harmonies of the Louvin Brothers still ring as loud and clear after all these years as they did when they were recorded. Every time I need a shot of heaven, I go and listen to 'You're Running Wild.' Then, I do."

Without much doubt, the most popular single Louvin song is "When I Stop Dreaming." In 1975 Charlie told writer Don Rhodes, "I think the song has earned some $2,000 a year for the writers for twenty years. It has been recorded by around ninety different artists, including Ray Charles, Don Gibson, and many others. In 1969 I was in Las Vegas in the audience watching Ray Charles in concert. He told the audience I had written 'When I Stop Dreaming' and had the spotlight put on me. It was one of the greatest moments of my life."

The artist who was most responsible for taking Louvin music beyond the boundaries of traditional country and bluegrass, however, was Emmylou Harris.

A native of Birmingham who grew up in the Washington, D.C., area, she got into the music during the folk revival of the 1960s and got her first break when she was asked to sing with folk rocker Gram Parsons. It was Parsons who had influenced the Byrds to move toward real country music and to do what is generally considered the first country rock album, *Sweetheart of the Rodeo*, in 1968. One of the more memorable tracks on the album was an ethereal reading of the Louvins' "The Christian Life." Harris soon learned that what so fascinated Parsons was Louvin harmony, and she began to add their songs to the duets she and Gram were doing. Before Parsons died unexpectedly in 1973, she had recorded "Cash on the Barrelhead" and "The Angels Rejoiced" with him. Harris soon had her own contract, and in the summer of 1975 she released her "career record," a single of "If I Could Only Win Your Love." It went to no. 5 on the *Billboard* charts and even crossed over into the pop charts. When she signed with the major Warner Brothers label in 1977, she began routinely including Louvin songs on her sets. She was also influential in getting other pop-flavored singers, such as Linda Ronstadt and Nicolette Larson, to record Louvin Brothers material. In 1979 she even did a duet with Charlie, "Love Don't Care," which managed to get onto the charts. In later years, Harris moved in an even more acoustic direction and continued her love of the harmony songs, and Louvin songs continued to play a key role in her music.

Curiously, when Emmylou Harris first came to Nashville and tried to find more Louvin Brothers records to listen to, she found that almost none of the classic albums remained in print. Capitol had kept available *The Family Who Prays* in an abridged form as a budget LP appealing to the gospel market, but none of the other two-hundred-odd originals were available to the general public. Drawing on her reputation and industry contacts, Harris was able to get the Country Music Foundation to go into their archives, get the Louvins originals, and make her a set of reference tapes. Similar things were happening all around the country in the 1980s: musicians and fans were circulating the Louvin music via their own homemade cassettes, drawn from fans who still had the old LPs or the purple-labeled Capitol singles. Dog-eared copies of *Tragic Songs of Life* were selling for up to fifty dollars a copy when they were to be found, and other Louvin albums moved on the collectors' market like blue-chip stocks. Capitol, the owner of most of the masters, seemed uninterested in reissuing them and unaware of the continuing interest in the Louvin sound. To remedy the problem, the Country Music Foundation in 1986 compiled a collection of "air checks" (recordings done live off the radio) of the Louvins performing on the air from 1951 to 1957, and watched it gain wide circulation in stores around the country. Rounder Records took a different series of radio shows the brothers had made in the early 1950s and released them as *Songs That Tell a Story*. They also managed to lease and reissue a set of the old MGM recordings. In 1989 another independent company, Copper Creek, found and released a concert tape of the Louvins at New River Ranch, an East Coast music park. Although each of the sets had its own shortcomings, they all helped keep the Louvin sound alive and to make it available to a new generation. Finally, in 1992, a prestigious firm from West Germany, Bear Family, managed to lease the Louvins' masters from Capitol. The result was a huge, eight-CD set containing every one of the Louvins' known commercial recordings and entitled *Close Harmony*. Carefully remastered from vault tapes and transferred through the latest digital technology, many of the recordings sounded better than they had on the original releases. A huge book that came with the set included dozens of pictures never before seen as well as a complete discography listing all the studio personnel and various issue numbers. Charlie Louvin cooperated with the producers and sat for long interviews in the preparation of the notes. (These notes, indeed, form the core of this present book.) In spite of a price tag that approached two hundred dollars, the set sold well, and serious singers and die-hard Louvin fans finally had a "collected works" to study.

It is not unusual to hear Louvin songs on the Grand Ole Opry stage or at any of the dozens of bluegrass festivals held today. Although Charlie himself is approaching retirement, there are several younger groups that specialize in the Louvin sound. Barry and Holly Tashian, whose work walks the edge between contemporary folk and country, have perfected the Louvin harmony and applied it to their own new songs. Barry, who began his career working as a harmony vocalist with Emmylou Harris, carried the tradition of Gram Parsons into the 1980s with a series of well-received albums. Even more devoted to the Louvin sound are the Whitstein Brothers, Charles and Robert, natives of Louisiana who grew up listening to the Louvins in the 1950s. In fact, their first album, a custom job also issued as an eight-track tape in 1978, was an entire collection devoted to Louvin gospel songs. By 1984 they had signed with Rounder and were releasing their own Louvin-style albums, such as *Rose of My Heart, Trouble Ain't Nothing But the Blues*, and *Old Time Duets*. Like the Louvins, the Whitsteins had the contacts and willingness to take their music into Nashville's commercial arena. Charlie Louvin supported their efforts and even asked Charles Whitstein to sing with him on certain tours and to cut a new tape with him, "Hoping That You're Hoping," in 1992.

There are other Louvins carrying on the legacy as well. Kathy Louvin, the daughter of Faye and Ira, who was only seven when her father was killed, had grown up as a little girl backstage at the Grand Ole Opry; her friends were figures like Bill Monroe and Roy Acuff and Hawkshaw Hawkins. In 1988 she gave in to her impulse to start writing songs and signed with the Nashville publisher Tillis Tunes. Before long she found her songs being recorded by Randy Travis, Dwight Yoakam, Patty Loveless, Martina McBride, and Ricky Van Shelton. In 1991 her "Keep It Between the Lines" became a major hit for Van Shelton. Kathy also developed her own singing style and through the 1990s made regular appearances in Nashville clubs and songwriter nights.

In the mid-1990s, the Louvin harmony and the Louvin songs remain part of the music of hundreds of country and folk and even rock singers. The intense Pentecostalism of some of the early gospel songs or the dated rock and roll of novelties like "Dog Sled" seem out of place for many today, but the sheer technical quality of Ira's songs and the full-throat harmony of the Louvin singing remain as fresh and vibrant as ever. At a time when classic harmony singing had almost died out in country music, Charlie and Ira brought it back, rejuvenated it, and showed how relevant it was to the very heart and soul of the music. When people like Ray Charles and Otis Redding and Aretha Franklin were injecting soul and passion and emotionalism into African-American music, the Louvins were injecting soul and passion into country music. Ira's songs themselves continue to surface in new arrangements and to find new fans. Many consider Ira to be one of the very best country songwriters, a master of prosody, vivid imagery, and perfectly turned phrases. A full study of his songwriting skill awaits another full book and a comprehensive collection of his canon.

APPENDIX:
LOUVIN SONGS RECORDED BY OTHER ARTISTS

Preliminary List of Louvin Songs Recorded by Other Artists

Title	Artist	Label	Rec. date	Rel. date	Louvins rec
Whispering, Now (Hill-Louvin)	Mel and Stan, the Kentucky Twins	Cap 40156		5-49	NO
Hard Road to Travel (I. & C. Louvin)	Red Sovine	MGM 10547		10-49	NO
Gonna Shake Hands with Mother Over There	Charlie Monroe	RCA 21-0345	3-50		NO
Take My Ring from Your Finger (ICL)	Johnnie and Jack	RCA 21-0448	10-50	3-51	NO
I'm Gonna Love You One More Time (ICL)	Johnnie and Jack	RCA 21-0448	10-17-50	3-51	NO
Bless Your Little Thumping Gizzard	Smilin' Eddie Hill	Decca 46212	8-22-49	1-50	NO
Your Address Unknown (ICL)	Roy Acuff	Col 20792	1-16-51	3-51	NO
Baldknob, Arkansas	Roy Acuff	Col 20804	1-16-51	5-51	NO
I'll Never Go Back					NO
West Virginia Polka	Wilma Lee and Stoney Cooper	Col 20861	7-13-51	9-51	NO
Are You Teasing Me?	Carl Smith	Col 20922	2-5-52	4-52	YES
God Saved My Soul	Carl Story	Mer 6404	3-6-52	7-52	NO
Are You Missing Me?	Jim and Jesse	Cap 2233	6-13-52	9-52	NO
Are You Afraid to Die? (CIL-Hill)	Carl Story	Mer 6413	8-3-52	9-52	YES
Land of Eternal Peace (CIL-Hill)	Carl Story	Mer 70603	9-52	4-55	NO
That's My Heart Talking					NO
I Just Love the Way You Tell a Lie (ICL)	Don Gibson	Col 21109	3-30-53	5-53	NO
Love and Wealth	Carl Story	Col 21137	6-1-53	7-53	NO

Title	Artist	Label			
Is Zat You Myrtle (ICL-Carlisle)	Carlisles	Mer 70174	-53	6-53	NO
Unpucker (ICL-Carlisle)	Carlisles	Mer 70232	-53	10-53	NO
Seven Year Blues	Webster Brothers	Col	-54		YES
Streamline Heartbreaker	Roy Acuff	Cap 2901	1-15-54		NO
Shake a Leg (ICL-Carlisle)	Carlisles	Mer 70351		4-54	NO
Mainest Thing (ICL-Carlisle)	Carlisles	Mer 70484		11-54	NO
Red Hen Boogie	McCormick Brothers	Hickory 1013		8-54	YES
When I Get the Money Made	Mac Wiseman	Dot 1236	2-53	2-55	NO
She Will Get Lonesome	Jimmy Collie	Hickory 1033		9-55	YES
On My Way to the Show	Carlisles	Mer 70712		10-55	YES
Ever-Ready Kisses	Country Pardners	RCA 6433	1-12-56	2-56	NO
I Take the Chance	Browns	RCA 6480		5-56	NO
A Man with a Plan	Browns	RCA 6730	7-27-56	11-56	NO
You Thought I Thought	Browns	Fabor 126	7-55	8-55	NO
Last Thing That I Want	Browns	RCA 6995	12-18-56	7-57	NO
As Long As You Love Me	Browns	RCA 6631		9-56	?
Television Set (Ira Louvin)	Cousin Jody N' Odie	Chic 1004		11-56	NO
Come and Knock (On the Door to My Heart)	Smiley and Kitty with Rita Faye	MGM 12381		12-56	NO
*Hot to Trot (Louvin and Lopley)	Andrews Brothers	MGM 12007		6-55	NO
Doubt	George McCormick	MGM 12592		12-57	NO

Continued

Preliminary List (continued)

Title	Artist	Label	Rec. date	Rel. date	Louvins rec
Wishful Thinking	Smiley and Kitty w/Rita Faye	MGM 12453		3-57	NO
You're in My Heart	Rita Faye	MGM 12551		10-57	NO
Because I'm Yours (But You're Not Mine)	Al Terry	Hickory 1075		3-58	NO
Stormy Horizons (Irene Franks-ICL)	Jim and Jesse	Epic 9508	12-7-60	3-62	NO
Five Days of Heaven (Louvin-Kershaw)	Osborne Brothers	MGM 13073	2-17-62	5-62	NO
I'm No Longer in Your Heart	Melba Montgomery	Nugget 605 N 2763		-62	NO
I've Learned to Live with You and Be Alone	Jean Shepherd	Cap 4915	10-26-61	3-63	NO
I'm Just Blue Enough (To Do Most Anything)	Little Jimmy Dickens	Col 41670	3-31-60	5-60	NO
A Message to Your Heart	Osborne Brothers	MGM 12762	2-59	3-59	YES
My Big John (ICL-J. Dean-Jimmy Newman)	Dottie West	Starday 574	11-61	12-61	NO
Cheatin' Is Catching (K. Wells-Ira L.)	Kitty Wells	Decca LP 4658	1-3-65	6-65	NO
Tip Toe	Judy Lynn	ABC/Pm 45-9767	12-15-56		NO
Thanks for Not Telling Me	Roy Acuff	Hickory 1113	8-27-59	12-59	NO
I Lost You After All (Ira L-H.Carter)	Jean Shepherd	Cap LP 1663	12-27-56	2-62	NO

—Compiled by Charles Wolfe and Eddie Stubbs

* also recorded by Terry Fell, RCA X-0149, released 7-55, as "I'm Hot to Trot"

SOURCES AND BIBLIOGRAPHY

The vast majority of the quotations from Charlie Louvin come from a series of personal interviews with the author during 1991, 1992, 1994, and 1995. These interviews were conducted in Nashville at various locations, and taped copies exist in the author's files. The most extensive interview sessions were those of October 6, 1991; December 11, 1991; April 20, 1992; and January 12, 1994.

Other quotations from Charlie have been taken from earlier articles by Don Rhodes and Douglas Green (see Select Bibliography) and the research of Alan Cackett. Additional information was drawn from Howard Miller's short book *The Louvin Brothers: From Beginning to End*.

I have also been permitted to draw information from a series of copyrighted interviews done with Charlie Louvin in 1990 by Stephen Plumlee and William Hogeland. Unpublished transcripts of these interviews are located in the files of Plumlee and Hogeland, who are currently developing a major film about the Louvins.

Data on the Sand Mountain gospel singing tradition (chapter 1) is partially drawn from my own research as well as three essays printed in *In the Spirit: Alabama's Sacred Music Traditions*, edited by Henry Willett (Montgomery, Ala.: Black Belt Press, 1995). The essays are Buell Cobb's "Sand Mountain's Wootten Family: Sacred Harp Singers," (40–50); Charles Wolfe's "Seven-Shape Note Gospel Music in Northern Alabama: The Case of the Athens Music Company," (62–80); and Joyce Cauthen's "Shape-Note Gospel Singing on Sand Mountain," (81–84). For a general background on the old-time fiddle and banjo contests that were so important to the Louvins' father, see Joyce Cauthen, *With Fiddle and Well-Rosined Bow: Old-Time Fiddling in Alabama* (Tuscaloosa: University of Alabama Press, 1989). This study is also the source for information and quotations about the Johnson Brothers band.

The history of duet singing in early country music is taken in part from the author's personal interviews with Bill Bolick (the Blue Sky Boys), with Bill Monroe (the Monroe Brothers), and with Lester McFarland (Mac and Bob). A good detailed account of the Louvins' special influences, the Delmore Brothers, is found in Charles Wolfe, ed., *Truth is Stranger Than Publicity: The Autobiography of Alton Delmore*, rev ed. (Nashville: Vanderbilt University Press, 1995). The quotation from the fan letter to Millie Good comes from a letter in the scrapbook of Millie Good McCluskey, interviewed by the author at her home in Cincinnati in April 1981.

The discussion of the Louvins in Chattanooga cames from interviews with Charlie as well as with Bob Douglas, leader of the Foggy Mountain Boys. Some of this material was published in Bob Fulcher's booklet of liner notes to the Tennessee Folklore Society's "Sequatchie Valley" LP (TFS-109), which also contains radio transcriptions that include the first known Louvin recordings. The quotation by Charlie Monroe is drawn from the oral history interview with him done by Doug Green in 1974, in the files of the Country Music Foundation in Nashville. There is little reliable material in print about Eddie Hill. A starting point is "Eddie Hill: A Big Man . . . with a Big Smile" in *Big Country News*, vol. 1, no. 2 (September 1969), 1–7. The author's attempts to interview Hill were only partially successful, but he was able to draw on research by Eddie Stubbs and conversations with Johnny Wright and Kitty Wells. For more details about the fad for atomic bomb songs in the late 1940s and early 1950s, see Charles Wolfe, "Nuclear Country: The Atomic Bomb in Country Music," *Journal of Country Music*, vol. 6, no. 4 (1978), 4–21.

For information about Lowell Blanchard and the Knoxville radio scene, see Charles Wolfe, *Tennessee Strings: The Story of Country Music in Tennessee* (Knoxville: University of Tennessee Press, 1976), and the liner notes booklet by Eddie Stubbs and Walt Trott, "Johnnie and Jack," BCD 15553. Data on the radio show "Songs That Tell a Story" are drawn largely from the liner notes by Doug Green to the Rounder LP of the same name, Rounder CD 1030.

In Chapter 6, information about Ken Nelson came from the author's telephone interview with him, September 11, 1989, and from similar interviews done by Stephen Plumlee (1991) and Rich Kienzle (1994) and shared with the author.

The background of the Grand Ole Opry in the 1950s as well as the early Nashville scene comes from the author's interviews with Louvin sidemen Paul Yandell, Jimmy Capps, George McCormick, Goober Buchanan, Johnny Wright,

Howard White, John Hartford, and Buddy Harman. Good basic background on the Opry itself can be found in Bill Malone's standard *Country Music, USA*, rev. ed. (Austin: University of Texas Press, 1985), and in Chet Hagan, *Grand Ole Opry* (New York: Henry Holt, 1989). The best account of the Browns and their relationship with the Louvins is the liner notes booklet to the comprehensive Bear Family CD of the Browns' work, BCD 15665 III, by Chris Skinker.

Other versions of the Ira Louvins–Elvis confrontation are given in Miller's book and in Peter Guralnick's *Last Train to Memphis* (Boston: Back Bay Books, 1994).

Details from the fatal car wreck in Missouri come from news coverage in the Nashville *Tennessean* (see Select Bibliography) and from discussions with Charlie Louvin. Information about Charlie's later career is drawn from interviews with him, from conversations with Ivan Tribe, and from Joel Whitburn's *Top Country Singles, 1944–1993* (Menomonee Falls, Wis.: Record Research, 1994).

The listing of additional Louvin songs recorded by others is based on my own research as well as that of Phillip Wells. Additional citations were provided by Gary B. Reid, Eddie Stubbs, Don Roy, and Richard Weize.

SELECT BIBLIOGRAPHY

"Bodies of Ex-Opry Star, Wife Returned Here." Nashville *Tennessean*, June 28, 1965.

"Charlie Louvin: He Just Does What He Does." *Cash Box*, 24 February 1990, 6.

Garbutt, Bob. "The Louvin Brothers." *Goldmine*, no. 58 (1981), 25.

Geno, S. L. "Charlie and Ira—the Louvin Brothers." *Bluegrass Unlimited*, vol. 17, no. 9 (1983), 12.

Green, Douglas. "The Louvin Brothers." *Bluegrass Unlimited*, vol. 7, no. 2 (1972), 6–9.

Guterman, Jimmy. "Sibling Revivalry." Boston *Phoenix*, 12 June 1987, sec. 3, 10–11.

Fulcher, Bob. "Sequatchie Valley: Seven Decades of Country Fiddling: Bob Douglas." Liner notes
    booklet to *Sequatchie Valley*, LP. Murfreesboro: Tennessee Folklore Society, TFS-109.

Miller, Howard. *The Louvin Brothers: From Beginning to the End*. N.p., n.d.

Rhodes, Don. "Looking Back on the Louvin Brothers." *Pickin'*, vol. 3, no. 2 (1976), 4.

Songs of the Louvin Brothers. Nashville: Acuff-Rose Publications, 1975.

"Still Riding High." *Country Song Round-Up*, no. 80 (1963), 6–7.

Wells, Phillip. *Songs by the Louvin Brothers Recorded by Other Performers*. Monograph. Bridgewater, N.J.:
    privately published, 1985.

Wolfe, Charles. *Louvin Brothers. Close Harmony*. Book to accompany Bear Family CD set
    BCD 15661 HI. Bremen, Germany: Bear Family, 1992.

———. "The Louvin Brothers: Ira and Charles." *Journal of the American Academy for the Preservation
    of Old Time Country Music*, no. 25 (February 1995), 9–11.

Most of the classic recordings that defined the legendary Louvin Brothers sound were made for Capitol Records between 1956 and 1963. Over the years, these original albums with their distinctive album covers and brilliant studio sound, have been cherished by fans and much sought after by collectors.

Capitol Nashville has embarked on a project to restore this legacy to print and to release key Louvin albums on compact disc. Digitally remastered and featuring detailed liner notes by *In Close Harmony* author Charles Wolfe, the initial discs (released in June 1996) include:

Satan Is Real (#37378)

A Tribute to the Delmore Brothers (#37379)

Tragic Songs of Life (#37380)

Look for these and future Louvin Brothers releases at your local record store.

For more information about these and other classic country releases on Capitol Nashville, write: Vintage Capitol Nashville, P.O. Box 22403, Nashville, TN 37202.

INDEX